Voices of CONSEQUENCES
ENRICHMENT SERIES

A Pursuit to a Greater "Self"

(12 Points to Establishing Good Character Traits)

By: Jamila T. Davis
Volume 3

VOICES
INTERNATIONAL PUBLICATIONS

Voices of Consequences Enrichment Series
A Pursuit to a Greater "Self:" 12 Points To Establishing Good Character Traits

Copyright © 2016 by Jamila T. Davis

This book is a nondenominational, faith-based instruction manual. It was created to inspire, uplift and encourage incarcerated women to overcome their dilemmas that led to their imprisonment, and to provide instructions to help them develop good character traits. The author shares the strategies she has utilized, both spiritual and practical, to correct her adverse character traits. This book in not written to promote any set of religious beliefs, although it does encourage readers to be open to receiving assistance for their "Higher Power," as they know Him.

The author does not claim to have originated any techniques or principles shared in this book. She has simply formulated a system of proven strategies, from her research and experience while incarcerated. A comprehensive list of references used to create this work is located in the back of this book. Readers are encouraged to use this list to obtain additional books to further their learning experience.

Printed in the United States of America. First Printing, 2016

LCCN: 2016943624
ISBN: 9780985580773

Voices International Publications
196-03-Linden Blvd.
St. Albans, NY 11412
"Changing Lives One Page at a Time."
www.vocseries.com
www.voicesbooks.com

Typesetting and Cover Design: Jana Rade (www.impactstudioonline.com)
Edited by: Dr. Maxine Thompson

TABLE OF CONTENTS

INTRODUCTION

Throughout the *Voices of Consequences* Series, we have learned some very important principles and strategies to achieve long-term success. This includes discovering our God-given gifts and talents. We have also learned how to sharpen our skill sets. Many of us have made tremendous progress and have tapped into our life's purpose. This is a great achievement, but it cannot be sustained without good character!

Good character is the key ingredient we need to stay rooted and grounded in life. It is the standard we can use that will help us stay on the right track. Character, when developed, forms our good habits that become one with us. It is the moral principles we live by that pave the way for our long-term prosperity.

Many people in the world have reached great heights of achievement, only to lose it! This is primarily because their success was not built on the strong foundation of character. Consequently, they missed the mark!

In this book, we will learn the importance of good character, discover the attributes of integrity, and learn how to cultivate them both. We will also examine real life examples that will help illuminate each lesson.

In our journey to restoration, it is important to fill ourselves with as much wisdom as we can. If we want to be successful, we must learn the techniques and strategies of successful people, then follow them. The road to empowerment is all about obtaining wisdom and knowledge. Wisdom is, "the what to do," and knowledge is, "the how to do it."

During my incarceration, I spent a great amount of time reading books, researching and studying the fundamentals to success. During my studies, I discovered successful people all have a common pattern. Their good fortune is not derived by luck; it is planned and purposed through their lifestyle and behavioral patterns. I also discovered there are universal laws and principles we must follow in order to gain and maintain prosperity. If we do not follow them, we will not succeed.

Learning these principles allowed me to take a close look at my own life and accurately pinpoint my errors. Bad behavior and bad habits only lead to one path—self-destruction. My goal in this book is to illustrate to you the grand importance of developing and sustaining moral integrity, as well as the consequences for not having it. I believe as you read this book, it will enlighten you to the root of your past problems. It will also help you develop the character you need to become victorious.

There is a great misconception in our world that talent alone equates to success. We are taught from youth to develop our skill sets, so we spend an enormous amount of time working on strengthening our gifts and talents. Sadly, though, we often neglect the key to sustaining long-term prosperity, which is developing our character. Like a rocket ship, many reach great heights of achievement because of our intense, concentrated efforts. We put our mind and our eyes on the prize and achieve it! We soar to the top, but are unable to maintain what we established. Think about it! Many of us have had good jobs, nice homes, beautiful cars, great companions and a significant amount of money at one time or another in life, only to have it all snatched away. The question becomes why?

Any house that is not built on a solid foundation will crumble! Yes, you can cut corners and build the house, but surely when the storm comes your house will fall down! You can fool yourself and others by the grand outward appearance of your home, but the storm will always come and reveal the true state of your structure.

Many of us have been in a race, all of our lives, to achieve success. We have gotten caught up in the hustle and bustle of this fast-paced world, developing crafty strategies to reach our ultimate goal. Some of us have even achieved the mark we sought after. We got a chance to stare at, hold, and temporarily gloat in our achievements, only to have the fruits of our labor taken away! This experience has taught us many valuable lessons. There are no short cuts in life! All short cuts will ultimately lead to destruction. The only way to achieve and sustain success is by building it on a solid foundation. Until we truly understand and accept this principle, life will ultimately be a constant roller coaster of ups and downs.

Crime only has one consequence—punishment! Whether it is today or tomorrow, it will catch up to you. Many of us have maintained a false belief that it is not our criminal behavior that caused our demise, but rather the strategy we used. Some falsely believe if we can find a craftier way to accomplish our crimes, we can, in fact, get away with it. This thinking is ignorant, and if it is maintained, it will ultimately lead to our destruction!

Crime does not pay! It always comes with some sort of consequence, even if it is not imprisonment; that is because it defies Universal Law. Always remember, the Biblical principle, you reap what you sow. (Galatians 6: 7-8). When we do bad things, or sow bad seeds, it will result in negativity in our lives. There is no way to get around it! Bad things will creep up on us unexpectedly because of the bad seeds we have sown. The only way to obtain a peaceful, prosperous life is to change our ways and our lifestyle. As we change, our quality of life ultimately changes too! There are no short cuts! As we work on "self" and improve our character, we will receive ultimate, long lasting success.

Taking the time out in prison to work on character can be great. We are in a unique environment that forces us to view life differently. When problems occur, we cannot just run away from them. In prison, we are confined to an environment that forces us to deal with our current circumstances. Living in an environment unwillingly with people of all different ethnicities and backgrounds allows us to see the behavior patterns of various people. Witnessing others and their dilemmas can be a great thing, especially when we come into the revelation that we do not want their fate to become our own. In this case, we can learn from those around us and equip ourselves not to make the same adverse mistakes.

Character is generally birthed in the midst of adversity. When life is all good, we don't believe we have a need to change. It is when we hit rock bottom that we surrender and look for a solution. It is at this very place where we can actually grow. Hardships and trials do not have to be a bad thing. They can become our opportunity for advancement. Time is very valuable! We must not let this time waste away! One of the greatest things we can do with our time is learn to work on "self." If we can utilize our imprisonment in a positive way, we can make up for lost time by going home and rising to the top!

So many people are walking around in the free world lost! They have no clue, which road to walk down or the way to true success. They are so caught up in people, places and things that they have missed the mark. Many of them will spend their entire lives miserable and die never achieving their purpose. Thank God for our mishaps, because that is no longer our fate! Now it's time to intensely work on our character, so when we reach our new-found success we can sustain it!

Through the lessons in this book, we will learn the secrets of the many successful people that have gone before us. They are no different from you and I. The only difference is they had the knowledge that we will now gain. Wisdom and knowledge equals power! Equip yourself today with the power to succeed!

Congratulations in reaching this point of achievement. You have now entered the doorway of great prosperity! Don't take this opportunity lightly. Utilize it to your advantage! May God open your eyes, create a new heart and renew a right spirit within you, according to His divine principles.

CHAPTER 1
A Heart Full of Love

One of the greatest attributes we can ever possess is a heart full of love. Love is the powerful force that radiates into the universe and brings us back an abundance of prosperity and joy. It is the energy of love that empowers us to succeed. God created us to become an expression of His love to one another. Without love in our hearts it is impossible to live life joyfully!

Love is a word that is used loosely by many. "I love you," is an expression that is commonly said. Unfortunately, many of us have no clue of what love really is! Love is not just a word; it is an action! True love is the genuine compassion and concern for another individual. Love is not bliss; real love is unconditional. It stands true, regardless of what another does in return.

Without the energy of love imbedded within our hearts, we become selfish and self-centered. Instead of getting caught up into achieving our God-given purpose on this earth, we become busy trying to satisfy our own selfish inner drive. Without love in our hearts, our thinking becomes contaminated. We stray away from the correct course in life and move on to the path of self-destruction. Many of us are in the position we are in today because of our lack of love.

For some of us, life has started off rough. Instead of being nurtured and loved, we have been beat down and abused by life, before we developed the skills to take care of ourselves.

Introduced to the venom of hate, we have encountered heartless behavior by others. As a result, we have suffered deep wounds because of these acts. Consequently, we have built up walls of protection around our hearts, which has caused bitterness and anger to settle in. As a means of protection, we have learned to survive by treating others the way that we were treated. Picking up the adverse behavioral patterns of others, we now stand as hurt people, who in turn have hurt others, not realizing our behavior only continues the cycle of hate. The only way to break this cycle is to learn how to love. As we begin to love again, we are able to tear down the walls of bad fate and destruction. As a result, our love channels a signal to the universe, which will disperse more love our way.

Removing our self-built walls of protection can be a difficult task. Deep inside many of us are frightened of being hurt again. We secretly made a vow that we would never put ourselves in a vulnerable position to be abused again. Therefore, we sustain our self-protection by any means necessary, which has caused extreme dissatisfaction. Based on our fears, we ruin relationships that threaten our self-made boundaries and we hurt people who genuinely love us. Blinded by fear, we are unable to discern what's real and what's fake. Consequently, we move through life repeating this cycle, ultimately draining ourselves and our loved ones, all because we fail to properly love ourselves and others.

In this chapter, we will explore the dynamics of love and its attributes. We will also learn how to effectively express unconditional love to others. This is a very important point in our road to change. Do not take the information in this chapter lightly!

Love is the most powerful force in the universe. Even the hardest heart can be pierced by the power of love. God

14

designed human nature to love. As innocent children coming into the world, we all have hearts open to love. It is not until we are defiled by life's turmoil that our hearts become bitter and hardened. When we become cold-hearted, we block the passageway of joy, happiness and prosperity. According to the Universal Law of Attraction, we get back the energy from the universe that we put out. Therefore, by becoming bitter and hateful to others, we generate those expressions to come back to ourselves. Now is the time to correct our adverse patterns! We must put out all the trash that has impaired us and stagnated our lives. By forgiving others who have done wrong to us, we take back control over our future. Love is ultimate empowerment. We are able to win every battle when we learn how to love!

As we previously discussed, one of the major misconceptions is what love truly is. Let's break the barriers of ignorance by exploring the characteristics that drive love.

Real love is an unconditional expression that is not based on what another person does. We are not to love a person in order to gain something; we love because that is one of our God-given tasks to do! Love is not selfish or self-centered. It is genuinely the whole hearted concern of another. Love is not jealous or deceitful. It has no hidden agendas or motives. Love is pure and kind. Love doesn't hurt, it helps. Love doesn't take away, it adds. Love looks for nothing in return, yet is sustains itself. Love isn't selfish, it is generous! Even when love is beaten down, or taken advantage of, it still never fails. Real love never disappears no matter what the other person does. This kind of love is called agape love, which is the love of God.

Despite all the wrong we may have done in life, God forgives us when we ask for His forgiveness and He never changes His love for us. God's love is powerful and unconditional! He created each of us to have this same type of love within our hearts. As we learn to love the way that God loves us, we open the doors for provision. As a result, we are no longer able to be hurt by people, because we don't expect them to compensate us. Instead, we look to God for our provision, and people, places and things no longer become our idols. As we love unconditionally, God will send people into our lives that will love us back the same way. As a result, our love becomes contagious, sparking even more encounters of love. The more love we give, the more love we will receive in return!

Loving others doesn't mean we have to be stupid or allow people to use us. God commands us to love others, as we love ourselves. That means we are to express our love, but, at the same time, care for "self." We are to help those who are in need, but we are not to enable people. We cripple a person when we do acts for them on a regular basis that they are equipped to do themselves. When we do for others what they should be doing for themselves, we actually harm them. Any injury we cause to an individual is not an act of love! We love people when we step back and allow them to take responsibility for themselves. Detaching, in this instance, is an act of love.

When you truly love someone, you want to see the best for that person, even if it doesn't benefit you. Real love is not about you; it is about the person you are loving. If you love a person based on what they will give you in return (even if it's just their love you are looking for), that is not true love. In this case, what you are looking for is called compensation. Many of us are hurt by people because we place a higher expectation on them than we should. Secretly, we have looked for that person to compensate us for our love. The best compensation we can ever get comes from God! Therefore, we must take our expectancy off of people and place our expectancy in God. He will never leave us or forsake us. Unlike people, God doesn't change. He is the same yesterday, today and forevermore!

I am not saying we shouldn't be disappointed by people's action, but we should never be hurt. Because we know whatever that person fails to give us, God will provide. For example, if a person leaves out of our lives, God will send a new person to enter. Understanding this principle, we know that God uses people as instruments to bless us. People are not our source of provision, God is! Just like God created us, He created them. Whatever we need in life to sustain, we must look to our Creator, and, in turn, He will lead us to the correct people, places and things that can help us. When we truly understand this revelation, people no longer have the power to hurt us. They may disappoint us at times. But even then, we can still rejoice, knowing we have God as our Partner, and He will send us new provisions.

Love is the expression of our worship, which honors God. As we honor Him by loving man, God, in turn, will honor us. Have you been loving others with the agape love that God intends us to love with, or have you been loving others with some sort of expectancy in return? Take a moment and analyze the relationships you have had with others who you believed you love, and analyze their relationships back to you. Ask yourself the following questions:

1) Did this love hurt?
2) Did this love add or did it take away?
3) Did this love expect something in return from you?
4) Did this love have your best interest at heart?
5) Was this love an expression of God's agape love?

Learning to truly love starts with loving "self." Remember, God commands us to love others as we love ourselves. Many of us have gone astray because we do not know how to love ourselves. Life's trials and tribulations have caused us to load ourselves with shame and guilt. These toxic emotions disable us and cause us to not feel worthy to be loved. In turn, it propels us to punish ourselves by inflicting self-hate, because we feel unworthy.

In the last two volumes of the *Voices of Consequences Enrichment Series*, we learned how to deal with our past and then let it go. We explored strategies and techniques to rid ourselves of shame and guilt. We also learned how to protect ourselves and learn to care for "self." Caring for "self" begins by loving ourselves, and realizing no matter what we have done in our past, God has forgiven us. He has given each of us a brand new slate. Regardless of what happened yesterday, we can start fresh today. We have all been blessed with the gift of life. Therefore, we must not stay stagnated by letting our past hold us down. Instead, we wipe off our defilement and look forward to the best, which is yet to come! Our real healing begins when we learn how to properly love ourselves.

Loving "self" is also expressing unconditional love. Regardless of what we do, or the mistakes we make, we must love ourselves the same. Each day we wake up and look in the mirror, we must tell ourselves, "I love you." Loving "self" means vowing to protect ourselves, at all cost. That includes, avoiding taking part in any activities that will ultimately cause hurt or harm to ourselves. Loving ourselves enables us to become our own best friend, lover and protector, all at the same time! We build up ourselves with nurture, care and reflection, (which builds up our self-esteem,) as we strive to reach our highest potential. As we learn to love "self," we treat others with the same expressions of love we would give ourselves. This makes life enjoyable.

We feel good inside because we have done the things for "self" we would want others to do for us. When we feel good, we are able to express our joy to others. As we master caring for "self" and loving "self," we ultimately learn how to become better lovers. As a result, we improve our relationships and bonds with others.

Love is powerful because it has the ability to block us from evil. When we continuously love others who lack love, eventually they will become broken down by love. Evil can never withstand or overpower love! We are commanded by God to love even those who hate us. This may seem foolish to some, but remember when we love with God's agape love, we aren't doing it to get something in return. Instead, we love that person to honor God. It is easy to love when you have no expectancy! When the one you love discovers the purity of your heart, and sees you have no hidden motives, your love will ultimately pierce their heart and cause that person to love back. Now that's powerful!

CHAPTER ONE- PART 2

Now that we understand the characteristics and the virtue of love, let's explore an example of love expressed in prison:

Sharon and Mary met each other in federal prison. Sharon is serving a 12-month sentence for tax evasion and Mary is serving a 48-month sentence for identity theft. Sharon, who is from Charleston, South Carolina, came from a good family, went to college and made an excellent living as a financial consultant. Blinded by the lure of money and prestige, she compromised by cheating on her income tax returns.

Mary grew up in a poor neighborhood in Chicago, Illinois. Life was tough for her in the inner city, so she sought a way to survive. Consequently, she turned to identity theft to help support her family. In a short period of time, Mary began to thrive in her new found lifestyle of glamour and local notoriety. Little did she know she would be betrayed by one of her closest friends, who had gotten caught in the department store opening up a fraudulent instant credit account. Mary's friend, facing imprisonment, decided to set Mary up to do business with a federal agent, which led to her imprisonment.

Sharon and Mary both handled their incarceration differently. Early on, Sharon came to terms of acceptance with her sentence. She did her best to make life as comfortable as possible in prison. Her family supported her throughout her incarceration. As a result, Sharon's family ties became very close.

On the other hand, Mary was very bitter about her incarceration. She always complained about her circumstances and her fate. Mary's family was very poor and could rarely afford to support her. She knew how to do hair well, so she used it as a means to hustle up enough commissary to make ends meet in prison. Sharon became one of Mary's hair clients, which is how the two women became friends.

Every time Mary did Sharon's hair, she would tell her about her mishaps and misfortunes. Sharon felt sorry for Mary and began to help her out. Sharon was an active Muslim woman, who attended Jumah services every Friday. Prison allowed Sharon to see her need to gain a closer relationship with her "Higher Power." As a result, Sharon began to study the principles of love and greatly wanted to shower her love on as many people as she possibly could.

Sharon began to share her spiritual findings with Mary. She often gave Mary cosmetics and commissary to help her out, even when she did not do her hair. As a result, the two women became good friends. Mary was even inspired to attend Jumah services with Sharon, because she desired to become just like her friend.

After Mary started attending services, she renewed her relationship with God. Shortly after, Mary's uncle wrote her in prison and began supporting Mary financially. Subsequently, Mary no longer needed Sharon's handouts and life became more manageable.

Sharon would often visit Mary and still express her love, but with her new found wealth Mary began to change. She no longer had time to do Sharon's hair. Instead, Mary started hanging out with a new crowd who befriended her for the things she could give them.

One day Sharon ran out of coffee and asked Mary if she would lend her some until she went to commissary. To her surprise, Mary was very rude and said she only had enough for herself. Sharon was disappointed in Mary's behavior, especially since she had shown her so much generosity in the past.

As time went by, the two girls ended up falling apart from each other. Despite this fact, Sharon always made it her business to speak to Mary in passing, even though Mary was now caught up with her new friends.

After a couple of months, Mary lost contact with her uncle. Consequently, she no longer had the money she had gotten accustomed to and her new-found friends began to separate themselves from her. Once again, Mary became very depressed and bitter about her life.

One day, after realizing that Mary was suffering from depression and lacked the things she needed, Sharon decided to put some items in her bag and she took them over to Mary's dorm. Mary began to cry as Sharon showed her expression of love, and she immediately apologized for how she had acted. Sharon gladly accepted her apology. Once again the two girls began to go to Jumah on Fridays together, just as they had in the past, and Mary's life circumstances became better.

Soon after the friendship resumed, Mary's grandmother began to help Mary out. This time around, Mary vowed to do the right thing. She offered to repay Sharon, who immediately declined her gesture. Yet, she encouraged Mary to help out others in her unit who were less fortunate. As Mary shared with other women in need, God, in turn, blessed Mary even more. Through this experience she learned the principles of love, sharing and giving.

Mary has completed her term of incarceration and is now applying these principles to her life in the free world. Sharon and Mary both completed probation successfully and they remain in touch with each other. Mary says Sharon's genuine love changed her entire life.

Now that you have read Sharon and Mary's story, I want you to stop and think about both Sharon and Mary and relate each character to yourself. Take a moment and answer the following questions:

1) Are you more like Sharon, Mary or both? In what ways?
2) Why was Sharon's friendship to Mary so powerful?
3) What do you think would have happened if Sharon totally cut Mary off?
4) Why was Mary so inspired to change her ways?

Now that we have analyzed an up close and personal example of unconditional love, let's explore how we can apply this standard of love in our own lives today.

When we begin to implement the practice of love into our lives, the first thing we must learn to do is always check our motives by asking the questions: Why are we giving our love to this person? And, what are we expecting in return?

When we love the way that God intends for us to love, we are to do so expecting nothing from man in return. Our priority should be pleasing God and doing the right thing, rather than to try and appease man. When we do things with no expectancy in return, we cannot be disappointed! If the receiver is ungrateful or unappreciative, that is their problem and not our own. God, in turn, will reward us, so we don't need that person's self-made reward!

When we learn to love as an act of homage to God, we also protect ourselves. We never allow a person to abuse us or use us. We only give what God puts in our hearts to do. The gifts that we give should never deprive us, hurt us or injure "self." We no longer get caught up in doing things to receive love. Instead, we give as an act of love, expecting nothing in return. If our recipients love us back, great; if not, that's okay, too. We now know if one door closes, God will, in fact, open a new door. Therefore, our lives are no longer governed by people, places or things, and we break the control others once had over us. As we change our ways and our thinking, our lives ultimately change for the better!

Each day we get up, we make "self" a priority. We do the best we can to allow our "self" to feel loved, becoming our own best friend, our lover and our protector. We protect ourselves by not allowing ourselves to take part in harmful activities. Instead, we cherish and honor our bodies by caring for them. We take the necessary steps to tap into our inner gifts and talents. In this journey, we discover purpose. Each day we live, we look for new ways to become a better "self." As we work on "self," we become whole. We no longer look for fulfillment by pleasing others. Instead, we do the best we can to please God.

Are you ready to restore your life by the power of love? Are you ready to witness the healing power that love awaits to give you? If so, say this short prayer request for love with me:

"God, I thank You for revealing to me the power of love. I desire to have the prosperous, peaceful life that love brings. I ask You to empty my heart of all defilement and negativity that blocks love from entering. Rain down Your love upon me and fill me until I am completely saturated in Your perfect love. Give me the strength I need to always express Your love, regardless of what others do to me in return. Keep me rooted and grounded in Your work and in Your principles. Each day, help me to become the person that You created me to be. When I go off track, gently nudge me and remind me of my purpose here on earth. God, my goal today is to become a perfect

expression of Your love. Help me to possess the tools I need to accomplish my mission. I receive Your help and Your guidance now, and I thank You for answering my prayers. Amen."

Congratulations! You have successfully embarked on the first destination in this journey. You have arrived at Destination Love! Continue with me on this journey, as we learn the other attributes of character we will need to sustain a successful life.

QUESTIONS

1) What is love?
2) Why is love so powerful?
3) Why do people often have a misconception of what love is?
4) Does love mean we are to neglect ourselves and let others abuse us? Why or why not?
5) When we love, who do we seek to please?
6) How do we get rewarded when we love other people?
7) Why do we need love to walk effectively in our purpose?

WRITING ASSIGNMENT

Write down four relationships you have in your life with others you love. Describe how these relationships are expressions of God's agape love or how they are not. Write out three ways you can change these relationships to become a better expression of God's agape love.

CHAPTER 2
The Solid Foundation of Honesty

We live in a society where words are used loosely and often not upheld. People make agreements and promises that they have no intention on living up to, making the words of our neighbors often baseless and void. We seldom know whom we can trust or not. As a result, we build up self-made walls of protection, making the choice not to trust anyone. At the same time, we follow the cycle of deceit by also using baseless words and making promises to others we have no intention of fulfilling. This cycle becomes destructive! Many of us believe it is, in fact, survival, but the venom of dishonesty poisons our hearts and can ultimately lead us to self-destruction. The only way to break the deadly power of deceit is to build our character based on honesty and integrity.

In this chapter, we will explore the attributes of honesty, as well as the consequences of being dishonest, and how it affects our entire lives. This chapter is very essential in our pursuit to a greater "self." Study the points and implement them into your everyday life. They will strengthen you and ultimately help you become a greater self!

In order to live a life of integrity, we must first be honest with ourselves. Then, and only then, can we be honest with others. Many of us have lived our lives in denial. We cover our true beings with distortion and make these false ideals into our reality. We live in glass houses, quickly able to identify faults in others, yet we cannot see our own true self. Instead, we mask ourselves to fit into society standards. Our actions are done to impress others. Consequently, we spend our whole lives trying to keep up with the Joneses; when, in actuality, the Joneses don't even live on our block! Then one day, we wake up and are left with the reality that those whom we admired and looked up to, thinking their world was much better than our own, are actually miserable. They, too, got caught up into chasing false fulfillment. They did what was necessary to obtain their goal, only to achieve it, and still not be satisfied.

On our journey to restoration, we must open our eyes, remove our masks, and be honest with ourselves about our current dilemmas. Denial only keeps us locked into darkness. It is acceptance and honesty that are our gateways to peace.

For many people it is hard to admit our own faults. It is human nature to blame others for our mishaps. Consequently, we resort to blaming someone else for the things we are responsible for. As a result, we stagnate our growth and never mature. We stay stuck in the same place in life, because we refuse to admit our own faults. We fail to grow, which causes us to remain miserable. Advancement in life cannot occur until we are able to be honest with ourselves. As we tear off the sheets of shame and guilt, we are then able to honestly reflect on "self." It is honesty that is the key ingredient which propels us into prosperous living.

At first, self-honesty may take practice and determination. When we consciously stop making excuses for inappropriate behavior, or adverse circumstances, we open the door for change. Therefore, we must open our eyes and view our circumstances for what they really are. Instead of being so quick to blame others for our dilemmas, we must stop and analyze what role we actually played in creating our own problems. When we are able to be honest with ourselves, it makes life easier. We no longer have to live a lie. Instead, we are free to be who we are and make adequate changes when necessary.

Living a dishonest lifestyle is tormenting! When you tell one lie, you have to continue telling other ones to keep your lie covered. Furthermore, you constantly have to look over your shoulder and behind your back, making sure no one exposes the truth. Lying is a trap for destruction. Once you commit to the lie, you become entrapped and entangled by it. The mask you cover yourself with will only force you to keep putting on a new mask to keep up your image. Therefore, you will never be at peace. Every time you think you can finally rest, you will be forced to tell another lie to maintain the status quo. This cycle constantly continues. Consequently, you will never be free or at peace, always fearing that your lie will be exposed.

Many of us have lived our lives in spiritual prisons long before we ever made it into the doors of actual imprisonment. We have chased the acclamations of our idols and did everything we could to gain recognition and attention. Consequently, we became the person we felt society wanted us to become, doing things to appease others, while denying our own true "self." Instead of facing the truth, some of us taught ourselves to believe our own lies. We've repeated them so many times to others that they have become one with us. This has caused further hardships.

Deep down inside we are now empty and void, trying to live up to a standard that is an illusion. Consequently, life has been miserable. We stare at ourselves in the mirror and feel hopeless, believing we are not good enough.

Well, it's time to pull off our masks and permanently throw them in the garbage! Today is a new day! We no longer have to be bound to dishonesty and deceit. Today, we are free to be ourselves. We are now ready to become the person God intended us to be! Our healing process has begun because we are finally able to be honest with "self." Therefore, we can now pinpoint our shortcomings and adequately fix them.

When we become honest with ourselves, we can easily become honest with others, because we are no longer governed by the emotions of other people. Instead, we are governed by God and our desire is to please Him. We tell the truth because we know that is what we ought to do! As a result, we live our lives in peace. Today, we don't have to recant our statements because they are factual. We have learned through life's mishaps that the truth will always prevail! Whether it be today or tomorrow, it has a way of floating to the surface at the time we least expect it. By telling the truth we no longer have to hide or be embarrassed by words that come back to bite us. As a result, we sleep well at night, and we are no longer tormented by deceit.

Compromise is the greatest trap for self-destruction. Many of us start off on the right track, but somewhere in the middle of us achieving our goal, we choose to compromise as a means to take a shortcut to reach our mark. We practice our deceit in darkness, hoping to never get caught. To soothe our conscience, we tell ourselves, "I'll just do this one time." Consequently, our compromising actions create a trap that drags us right back to our starting point! Whatever we gain from deceit or dishonest practices will always be taken away from us! It will never last. The very thing we thought we got away with will come back to bite us in the end!

It is important to understand that compromise is never worth it. Think about the crime that led to our imprisonment. Had we not placed ourselves in certain predicaments, we would not have had to suffer the consequences. The lesson we all learned the hard way is: Compromise always comes with consequences! There is no way around it! Remember the Universal Law of Attraction. We reap in life the seeds we sow. Therefore, if we are dishonest and deceitful, we open the doors for negative things to happen to us. The consequences for our actions can come in many forms, which often are unexpected. When you add up the cost, or the price we have to pay for our adverse behaviors, it always equates to more than what we stood to gain. Think about your imprisonment and those who have to suffer because of your wrong choices, including yourself. Now honestly ask yourself the question, "Was it worth it?" Had you just taken your time and done things differently, you could be living a great prosperous life and would not have to suffer any punishment.

It is important that you think before you act. Before you take actions, ask yourself the questions: "What consequences could I reap as a result of my actions?" And, "Is there another course I should take?" Mature people weigh the costs before they act. It is time for you to become mature. The only way to avoid unwarranted trials and tribulations is to hold standards of integrity at all times, regardless if someone is watching or not. When you set standards of integrity and follow them, they will protect you from falling into the traps of evil and darkness. Ultimately, they will become the fence that keeps you on the right track.

It is important that we drill in our minds the fact that there are no shortcuts in life! No matter how good opportunities may seem, if we cheat the system and compromise our integrity, it will always cost us more than what we stand to gain. We cannot move forward in life until we realize the truth of this revelation. Think about all the times you did something in life, thinking you would get over. Now think about the cost you had to pay for your actions. Honestly ask yourself,

"Was it worth it?" Remember, you always reap what you sow! If you rob someone, someone will rob you or somebody whom you love. If you lie to someone, someone will lie to you, too. If you cheat someone out of something they deserve, someone else will cheat you. When you understand this universal principal, you will see that we have in fact set the standards for our lives based on our own actions. The only way to break the chains of adversity is to live life with integrity. There are no exceptions!

Let's explore some examples of honesty and compromise to gain an up close look at the results of each.

EXAMPLE 1

Lisa and Katherine were best friends since grade school. They both grew up together in South Central, Los Angeles. Life growing up for the girls was rough, but they managed to stay on track and graduate from high school. Lisa had dreams of making it big one day and becoming a lawyer. Katherine also had big dreams. She wasn't sure of exactly what she wanted to do, but she knew she desired to be wealthy.

After graduating from high school, Lisa immediately went to college and Katherine followed Lisa's lead. The two girls struggled to pay their own way through school. At times, they had little to nothing to eat, but they pushed ahead. All was well until one day Katherine, turned off by her financial struggles, decided to quit school and get involved in doing credit card schemes.

Despite Katherine's absence, Lisa continued with her studies. For many years, she struggled to get through college and law school. She often sacrificed and did without to reach her goal. On the other hand, Katherine lived a lavish lifestyle, without putting forth much effort. For many years, she was

32

able to cheat her way to the top, and she was successful at it. Katherine drove a Mercedes Benz, bought herself a new home and had all types of designer clothes and jewelry. According to society's standards, Katherine had made it!

Lisa contemplated many times following Katherine's path and giving up on her dream. But something deep down inside of her wouldn't allow her to quit. As a result of her drive, Lisa successfully completed law school and became a federal prosecutor. Meanwhile, Katherine continued to maintain her illegal lifestyle for many years. She was always very smart and cautious about her surroundings, so she successfully avoided getting caught.

One day, Katherine met a man named Darrell who was a big time drug dealer from the neighborhood. Katherine was attracted to Darrell's power and money, and Darrell was attracted to Katherine's "go getter" mentality. The two of them became romantically involved and Katherine let Darrell move into her home in the suburbs of Woodland Hills.

At first, life was grand for the two lovers. Darrell enjoyed living outside of the hood, and Katherine adored the admiration and attention she got from Darrell. The couple continued to live their separate illegal lifestyles; Darrell sold his drugs and Katherine did her credit card schemes. Together the money they made was very good! Katherine's knowledge and know-how helped Darrell step up his game. She helped him buy a brand new Range Rover and a BMW. As a direct result, Darrell's' notoriety in the neighborhood soared and he became the envy of other local drug dealers.

Darrell had a good friend named Raheem, with whom he often did drug deals. Raheem became very jealous of Darrell's new-found celebrity status in the hood, so he decided to set Darrell up. Raheem called the crime tip line and gave them intricate details about Darrell's illegal organization. Consequently, the Feds began to watch Darrell.

* *While the Feds investigated Darrell's drug activities, they ran across Katherine and became more intrigued with her complex white collar credit card schemes. As a direct result Darrell and Katherine both became targeted by the Feds, and they were each charged with Conspiracy to Sell and Distribute Crack Cocaine, Identify Theft and Credit Card Fraud.

Indicted on RICO charges, as their organization appeared to be intertwined with drugs and fraud, Katherine was distraught! Coming out of the court room after her arraignment, shackled and in handcuffs, Katherine ran into her old friend, Lisa, who was now a federal prosecutor.

Lisa had Katherine taken into a holding cell in the basement of the courts. When the door closed, the two friends began to cry and weep together. There wasn't much Lisa could do, but she told the arresting agent her affiliation to Katherine, and gained Katherine the favor of the courts.

In the end, Katherine's case was severed from Darrell's and the RICO charges were dropped. Yet, she still had to pay the price for her illegal life style. Katherine was sentenced to fifty months in Federal prison for identity theft and credit card fraud. She lost her house, cars and money, and was forced to start her life all over from scratch.

Katherine came home from prison with nothing. She reached out to her friend, Lisa, who had since become a State Judge, living a very prosperous life. Staring directly at the difference of how her life turned out compared to Lisa's life, Katherine recognized her costly mistake of compromising her integrity, and greatly regretted not finishing school.

Looking at Lisa and Katherine's story, does it remind you of yourself or some of your peers? Katherine seemed to have a head start in the beginning, but, in the end, her compromising actions crept up to bite her, and led to her downfall. On the other hand, Lisa maintained her focus, struggled to make it through law school, and turned out to become a successful Judge. Katherine's hardships and her bruises taught her compromise just doesn't pay! Lisa's lifestyle of hard work and integrity was the better choice. She will be able to sustain everything she worked hard for. She doesn't have to look behind her back, and she can sleep well at night!

EXAMPLE 2

Gina worked hard and paid her way through school. She became a certified accountant and opened up an office in Richmond, Virginia. Gina's business quickly began to take off. During tax season, she made more money than she ever dreamed. As a result, she rewarded herself by splurging, living a lifestyle comparable to others who were well seasoned in her field.

Gina didn't realize after the tax season her money would not come in as fast. Consequently, after the prosperous months ended, she struggled to pay the new debts she had taken on. Gina loved her new lifestyle and was now threatened to lose it. The fear of losing what she gained crept in, and she began to think of ways she could sustain the material items she had already obtained.

Believing she could get away with fraud, Gina began to make up and file phony tax returns, using the stolen information of mentally retarded people. The money began to roll in and she thought she could finally relax. Gina used the illegal money she made to pay off her debts. Then, she stopped her illegal activities. Directly following, things appeared to be back to normal. Gina learned how to budget and manage her money and she vowed to never do anything illegal again.

Shortly after, Gina gained a large client who she began to do accounting for. Their dealings went well, until the president of the company decided to cheat Gina out of her fees. He owed her several thousands of dollars for her hard work, which Gina had already accounted for in her personal budget, most of which was pre-spent.

After not being successful in collecting the past debt, Gina had to take the company to court to collect her well-deserved money. Gina was surprised when the company counter-sued her and claimed she, in fact, defrauded them. The lawsuit turned into a long legal battle that cost Gina even more money and an enormous amount of time. She was also investigated for being a part of fraudulent activities that thecompany alleged. Directly following, the I.R.S. swarmed Gina's office. They determined she wasn't guilty of any fraud to the company, yet they found the fraudulent tax returns Gina prepared for the mentally retarded people who weren't her real clients.

Gina was prosecuted and charged with tax fraud. She pled guilty and was sentenced to twenty four months in Federal prison. Consequently, she lost her license to practice accounting, and during her imprisonment, she lost her business and her home. Gina now sits in a 5 1/2 x 9 jail cell, just like you and I, and she greatly regrets her decision to compromise her integrity. Today, she realizes it just wasn't worth it!

Gina started off on the right track. She did what was necessary to establish herself, but bad budgeting and wrong choices led her to compromise. This ultimately caused her own self- destruction.

When we get out of prison, we must make sure we stay on the correct path. If not, we can end up just like Gina. One bad choice to compromise caused her to lose everything she worked hard for. In Gina's case her punishment wasn't right away. She thought she had gotten away with her crime, and even chose not to do it again. In the end, that didn't matter! She still had to pay the price for what she did. Gina sowed a bad seed by cheating the I.R.S. and the mentally retarded people whose information she used. In turn, she reaped the consequences by attracting a bad client who cheated her out of her well-deserved pay. Gina's mishaps happened in accordance with the law of attraction. She reaped what she sowed, and in a worse way than what was dealt out! That is why we must always be careful of our actions. By setting high standards of integrity and always being honest, we close the door to future mishaps.

Now that we understand the importance of honesty, and the consequences of deceit and compromise, we each have a choice to make. Will we change, or will we remain the same? The choice is ours!

If you are ready to change your lifestyle and live according to principles of honesty and integrity, follow me in this prayer:

"God, I thank You today for revealing to me the importance of honesty. I realize I must always be honest in order to live a prosperous, peaceful life. Now I ask You to give me the strength, the courage and the ability to always be honest. My desire is that the words I speak out of my mouth will always be pleasing in Your sight. Lead me and guide me onto Your desired path for my life. Help me to recognize when I do things that are displeasing to You. As I am honest, please allow me to reap the benefits that honesty brings. Send people into my life who will also be honest and integral to me.

I thank You now for empowering me with the gift of honesty. I receive it and will walk on the path of honesty all the days of my life. Amen."

Congratulations! You have made another huge step in the pursuit to a greater "self." Go back and review the points in this chapter. Don't take the information you've gained lightly. Apply the principles of honesty and integrity into your everyday life today!

QUESTIONS
1) Why is honesty important?
2) What is self-honesty?
3) Why do people suffer if they refuse to be honest with themselves?
4) What is compromising behavior?
5) Why does compromising behavior lead to self-destruction?
6) Why is living a lie tormenting?
7) Why is it hard at times to tell the truth?

WRITING ASSIGNMENT
Write down three times in your life where you told a lie and how that lie effected you. Then, write down a time when you weren't honest with yourself and what the results were for your mistake. Last, write down a time in your life where you compromised your integrity, how it made you feel, and what the ultimate result was.

CHAPTER 3
Protected by Loyalty

We live in a world where many people are self-centered, only looking to satisfy themselves and their own desires. In the race to self-satisfaction, people often step on, misuse or hurt others to get to their desired destination. When this happens, people turn bitter and heartless, and cycles of distrust and usury become the norm. As we are inflicted by deceit and betrayal from others, we are enticed to take part in the same cycle in order to secure our own self-interests. Consequently, this destructive pattern never ends! We misuse and hurt others; in turn, someone else misuses and hurts us.

However, we cannot go on living life in this crazy, unethical manner! Taking charge of our lives means we break this destructive cycle and set high standards of integrity. As a result, we become loyal to ourselves and others.

In this chapter, we will learn the importance of loyalty, and how our loyalty affects others. One of the greatest character traits a person can possess is loyalty. True loyalty is rare, and those who possess it are well sought after! The goal of this chapter is for each of us to examine the contents of our own hearts, remove the defilements that have kept us self-centered, and develop the attributes of loyalty.

One of the biggest struggles people in the world have is the willingness to commit to something or someone. Human nature is to be in control. Therefore, we desire to remain free spirits. This causes us to move about life only doing the things that bring satisfaction to us, sometimes neglecting our commitments to others especially if it imposes on our self-satisfaction. Few really know what it is to be loyal to others. The only loyalty many people hold is to themselves. Consequently, betrayal is rampant and many never take note of the pain it inflicts on others.

Loyalty is the foundation of all relationships. Without loyalty there can be no trust. If we can't trust one another we remain isolated in self-made walls of protection, which is also a form of imprisonment. This isolation prevents us from achieving God's purpose for our lives.

Loyalty is the ingredient that brings trust, comfort and protection into our relationship with others. It is a necessary prerequisite to any friendship. Loyalty is the expression of love we give to others that lets them know our deeds are genuine. It is the force that uplifts our brothers and sisters when they are down. Loyalty lets them know they can trust us and confide in us, and we will not harm them. Loyalty is the gate key that opens the bars of self-made prisons people have built for protection.

Loyalty is commitment. It says, "Regardless of what we go through or what you have done, I have your back." Loyalty withstands the test of time. It is not just there to enjoy the good times and get all it can while the going is good; loyalty stands faithfully through the good and bad times. It remains true, for better or for worse.

Loyalty is the stripe of dignity that shows what moral fibers that our character consists of. The light of loyal people shines brightly for the world to see! Loyal people are the ones that are eventually rewarded. When they stay steady during the rainy season of life, they receive their prize when the sunny season comes.

Loyalty has no motive. It protects the interest of the one whom it is loyal to, and it genuinely wants to see the best happen for that person. Even when loyal people are hurt and harmed by others, they stand true. That does not mean loyal people are ignorant or stupid. They are smart people who set boundaries, which protect them from allowing others to harm or put them in danger. Loyalty is wise to simply detach during certain seasons, giving time for the person to recognize their faults. Loyalty doesn't disappear even when it detaches. It still peeps in from afar and waits for the right timing to grab the hand of its recipient, and stands ready to pick them up if they fall. Loyalty is a grand expression of unconditional love. It says, "regardless of what happened, I forgive you and I love you because I am loyal."

The standards of loyalty are high. Many people believe they are loyal, but their heart and their actions do not measure up. Loyalty is tested by the fire and storms of life. It is hard to see who is loyal when you are experiencing good times. Everyone likes a party, so even our enemies will show up to a celebration. When rough times come, we are able to see who is, and who is not, loyal. When there is no longer anything to gain, disloyal people walk away. There is no reason for them to stick around at that point, so they depart. When you no longer have anything to give or offer, loyal people remain by your side. Their expression of love shows you they have no hidden agenda. These people love you for who you are, and not for what they can get! This is one of the greatest expressions of love one can give.

Our first commitment of loyalty should be to God. He is the One who has blessed us with life and is always faithful to us, regardless of what we do! Our disloyalty can be seen most clearly when we examine our loyalty to Him. Many of us only come to God when we are down or experiencing hardships in life. When things are good we forget about the One who has enabled us to receive the pleasures of that season. When all is well, we often turn our back on the very Source of our joy. This is the biggest example of disloyalty.

When we are disloyal to God we stop up the flow of our blessings. Our hearts become defiled, disabling us from receiving from Him. At this point, God uses hardships and tribulations to enlighten us to our adverse behavior, causing us to return back to Him.

The first step in developing loyalty is strengthening our commitment and loyalty to God. One of the first things we should do before we start our day is thank God for life and spend time with Him in prayer and meditation. This duty is a necessary prerequisite to living an abundant life. We need God to function. He is now our Partner and our Friend, so we must treat Him as such. God deserves to be highly prioritized. Our relationship with Him is the most important relationship that we can have. Therefore, we should honor God by being loyal to Him. Loyalty to God consists of seeking Him daily for strength and guidance, not just during the bad times, but also in the good times, too. Seeking God should become a habit that is one with us.

Unlike people, God doesn't easily give His trust away. God tests each of us to see the level of our commitment and loyalty. In His testing seasons, He uses the fire of adversity to see our reactions. Those who stand and are loyal to God, even in the midst of adversity, ultimately pass God's test and are rewarded. Many of our dilemmas are simply a test. Has God given you a test that you now realize you have failed? Don't fail any more of God's tests! You can pass each one by girding yourself with the coat of loyalty.

Our loyalty to God is our protection from evil and hidden agendas. When we train ourselves to be committed to maintaining integrity, regardless of our circumstances and situations, we will not compromise. As a result, when we train ourselves to be loyal, we ultimately become the person God created us to be. Our bright light shines to the universe, causing others to shine their bright light on us, and loyalty becomes our footstool that propels us to unimaginable levels!

When we are loyal to others, we become walls of protection to them. Loyal people do not allow any harm to come to those whom they are loyal to. Loyal people do not hurt others; instead, they protect them. If someone comes along who tries to slander or hurt the one loyalty protects, it stands up and defends that person. Loyalty doesn't join in attacks or talk about the one whom it is loyal to. If that person does something that is wrong, loyalty waits until the appropriate time and pulls the individual to the side and lovingly tells them about their faults. Loyal people don't use and abuse others. Instead, their loyalty sees what can be added or brought to the table. Even when a person has nothing else to give in return, loyalty still shows up on time, and helps that person in any way it possibly can.

Loyalty is solid; it doesn't float back and forth. Loyalty stands strong at all times, right, wrong and indifferent. Yet, loyalty doesn't promote bad or compromising behavior. Instead, it lovingly guides, heals and protects its receiver from harm. Loyalty doesn't hurt; it helps and soothes all pain. It is not selfish or self-centered. Just as it cares for "self," loyalty always thinks about the best interest of others.

Now that we discussed the characteristics of loyalty, let's think about our current circumstances and conditions and about those who have stood with us through this rainy season, proving to be loyal. How does the loyalty of your friends and family members in this season make you feel? Have you been as loyal to them as they have been to you? Is there anyone in particular whose loyalty surprises you? What can you do to become a more loyal person when you get out of prison?

Asking yourself these questions helps us see the effects of loyalty and how we can become more loyal to others. Loyalty is the character trait that helps us to heal and achieve complete restoration.

God created each of us to be loyal people. It is His desire that we stand, protect and encourage others, especially when they are down. One of the greatest ways we can honor God is by being loyal to the people He places in our lives.

People often use the word friendship loosely. When you say to someone you are their friend, with your mouth you are making a commitment to be loyal to that person. Your words say, "Through thick or thin, I've got your back. I won't ever hurt or harm you intentionally. I will be there for you and protect you at any chance I get. I will lift you up and encourage you when you're down. Even when rough times come, I won't hide my face from you. Instead, I will be the person who offers you a cup to drink from and encourage you to push ahead. I will not take from you or misguide you. I will give you whatever I have to offer. In addition, I will give you good advice and always be honest with you. If I see that you are headed in the wrong direction, I won't turn my back on you; instead, I'll gently grab your hands and lovingly warn you of the danger ahead. No matter what storms come our way, I promise, I'll be there. You mean a lot to me, that's why I have chosen to call you my friend. Friend, I love you."

This is a powerful statement. If you are not willing to make this type of commitment to a person, do not call them a friend; they are simply an acquaintance. Friendship comes with the commitment of loyalty. Without loyalty, there is no friendship!

Loyalty is not easy; it takes work to develop! We must constantly examine our motives. Do I have my friend's best interest at heart? Am I secretly looking to gain something from my friend? Are my actions pure hearted? As we ask ourselves these questions, we can realign our motives and remain pure hearted in our actions.

Now that we have examined loyalty and its attributes, let's take a look at two examples of disloyalty and loyalty.

EXAMPLE 1

Sally grew up in a middle-class suburban neighborhood in New Jersey. As a little girl, she lacked the love and attention she so desperately sought after from her mom. Sally's mom felt that having Sally ruined her "good years." Her mom secretly resented Sally and treated her harshly at times.

Sally couldn't wait until she was grown to get out of her mother's house. She married her high school sweetheart, as a way of escape. Unfortunately, her husband became abusive, so she split and got a divorce.

Stuck with nowhere to go, Sally moved back in with her parents. Yet, Sally's mom never changed her controlling ways. As time went by, Sally began to date a new man, named Jim, who her mother disliked. Torn between her mother and the man, Sally chose the man. He became her second husband and she started her life over with him.

Once again, separated from her parents, Sally made Jim the priority of her life. She had a good job and worked hard while Jim enjoyed the convenience of his seasonal construction jobs. Sally footed most of the weight as her income exceeded

Jim's, yet she didn't mind. She enjoyed Jim's attention and secretly liked the fact she had someone who depended on her. Sally's work and her money gave her a sense of pride, making her feel significant. The more that she gave Jim, the more she believed he would love her.

One day, Sally got a call from Jim's boss. Jim had stolen over $20,000 from his boss's credit card and he threatened to put Jim in jail. Sally pleaded to his boss and promised to repay the debt. To resolve the matter, Sally picked up a second job as a waitress to help pay back Jim's debt. She even gave up her nice apartment to lessen the bills and insure Jim's boss got paid quickly, all to keep Jim from going to jail.

Jim had a child from a previous marriage whose mother began abusing drugs, so Sally opened her doors to Jim's son. She even fought through the courts to get him back from Child Care Services' foster care division. After several months of court hearings and thousands of dollars in legal fees, Sally got Jim's son back, and she was finally happy. At last, Sally had the family she always wanted, but after Jim's son moved in, the bills increased in the household.

Threatened to lose the lifestyle the couple was accustomed to, Jim taught Sally how to steal money from the company she worked for, without being detected. At first, Sally was reluctant, as she wasn't comfortable with committing a crime, but after Jim's pressure and the thought of winning his love, Sally compromised. She wrote several checks out of her boss's account, which Jim helped her to cash.

Nevertheless, after stealing the money, things didn't get better, as Sally expected; they got worse! Using the money Sally gave him, Jim caught the attention of another woman who made more money than she did, and Jim secretly began to cheat. He only intended to use this new woman, but as time

46

passed, he fell in love. Jim wanted to be with the woman, but he did not know how to get Sally out of the picture.

Madly in love with the new woman, Jim contemplated a way to remove Sally out of his life, so he decided to go to her job and tell the boss about the fraudulent checks she wrote. Immediately, Sally was fired and her boss pressed charges. As a result, Sally was locked up and convicted of third degree charges for theft by deception.

Sally was devastated when she got her legal discovery documents and learned her own husband had set her up! This caused her severe depression. In her mind, she believed imprisonment was the worst thing that could happen.

In prison, Sally renewed her relationship with God, and, for the first time. she began to work on "self." She asked God for forgiveness for her sins and to help her to experience a new abundant life.

Sally was facing five years, but the Judge decided to have mercy on her. After serving six months in prison, she was sentenced to time served and probation.

Today, Sally works with women who battle with low self-esteem. She empowers them with information on how to love themselves. Sally is happy and working in her purpose. Recently, she met a new Christian man whom she dates; the couple is looking forward to getting married. Sally refuses to rush anything. She is keeping herself focused and allowing God to reveal if this new man is right for her. For the first time in Sally's life, she finally feels fulfilled. Working in her purpose brings her no greater joy!

Example 2

Tyeisha grew up in the city of Detroit, Michigan. After graduating, she married her high school sweetheart and had five children. Her husband, Dwayne, held a good job, driving city buses, while Tyeisha stayed home and raised the kids.

Oftentimes, Dwayne worked overtime to take care of all the family bills. As a result, Tyeisha was lonely many nights and often grew bored.

Dwayne had a cousin named Keith, who lost his job and became homeless. Dwayne allowed Keith to stay in his guest room until he got back on his feet.

Keith began to spend a lot of time with Tyeisha while Dwayne was at work. He was good to Tyeisha and her kids, often taking them out to eat and to the movies with the money he got from his unemployment checks. After spending time with Keith, Tyeisha began to feel good again, just like she did in her younger years.

Quickly Keith and Tyeisha grew very close and, on one unexpected night, they started to have a romantic affair. They both tried to conceal their relationship from Dwayne, until Tyeisha discovered she was pregnant. Deciding not to have an abortion, she packed her clothes and left with Keith.

One day Dwayne came home from work and found his oldest child caring for the children and all of Keith and Tyeisha's stuff gone. Tyeisha left Dwayne a confession note, saying she was sorry and she had to go. Dwayne was deeply hurt, but he was determined not to let his children suffer.

Dwayne moved his mother up from Alabama and she came to care for the children. Dwayne's mother kept the family together and got everyone active in the church. The messages of the pastor kept Dwayne sane and gave him the drive to go on, even though he greatly missed his wife.

Tyeisha and Keith moved in to a small rooming house on the south side of Detroit. Keith had a secret habit of smoking crack. As time went on, Keith convinced Tyeisha to get high with him. Reluctantly, she tried crack to appease him and she enjoyed it. The drug was addictive and quickly became her new best friend, so much so that she started stealing and even selling her body to keep up with her habit.

Tyeisha was seven months pregnant when she looked in the mirror and couldn't stand to see her reflection anymore. She cried out for God to help her and asked Him to forgive her for all the wrong she had done. Moments after she cried, lying on the floor of the crack-infested apartment where she and Keith rented a room, the cops ran in the house and locked everyone up for possession of crack cocaine.

Inside her lonely prison cell, once again, Tyeisha began to cry out to God. She didn't know what to do and had no place for her baby to go. Dwayne read about the drug bust in the newspaper and saw Tyeisha was arrested. Upon finding out the news, he immediately went to the county jail to check on his wife. Tyeisha was surprised to get a visit. She had no real family and didn't have a clue who would be coming to see her.

Tyeisha's heart dropped when she discovered it was Dwayne who was her visitor. Dwayne smiled with joy as he greeted his wife, whom he missed dearly. His genuine compassion and concern pierced Tyeisha's heart and the couple reconciled.

Dwayne supported Tyeisha through her imprisonment. He and his mother even came and got the baby after Tyeisha gave birth in jail. Dwayne cared for and loved the baby as if it was his own.

While imprisoned Dwayne forgave Tyeisha for all the wrong she had done and encouraged her to renew her relationship with God. Dwayne's kind heart and loyalty sparked change within Tyeisha. She is now out of prison and back raising her family. She has been drug-free for over five years! Tyeisha recently obtained her drug treatment counselor's license. The unconditional love Dwayne showed her, she now passes on to the clients she helps at the Drug Rehabilitation Center where she works at. Tyeisha is determined to do the best with her second chance at life!

These two stories illustrate the power of love, loyalty, dishonesty and betrayal. I want you to take time out and analyze each example. What character closely fits with your own personality? How powerful was the love these characters displayed? How powerful was the disloyalty these characters displayed? Reflect on your answers and decide which character traits you would like to develop and dethrone.

Now that you know the virtue of loyalty and friendship, are you ready to become a loyal person? If so, please follow me in this prayer:

"God, thank You for allowing me to see the depth of true loyalty and its importance. I now desire to be a more loyal person. Give me the heart and desire to always be loyal to the people I commit to. Teach me how to love and be loyal. Help me to stay mindful of the needs of others around me. Allow me to be a protector and a giver to those I am loyal to. Let Your light shine brightly through me to inspire others to produce their best. Awaken my spirit to know when I am not being loyal and give me the help I need to change my course. Most importantly, help me to always be loyal to You! I thank You for Your divine strength, insight and help. I now receive it and I decree and declare to the universe, 'I am loyal!' Amen."

Congratulations! You have made another huge step in the pursuit to a greater "self." The new strength of your loyalty will allow you to soar in life and take you places you never dreamed or imagined you could go! Today, you have indeed become a better person!

QUESTIONS

1) What does it mean to be loyal?
2) Why is loyalty important?
3) Who should our most important relationship of loyalty be to? Why?
4) Why do many people struggle with being loyal?
5) What is the role of a real friend?
6) How can we work on becoming more loyal?
7) How do you stay loyal, yet at the same time care for "self"?

WRITING ASSIGNMENT

I . Write out three experiences when others have expressed true loyalty to you.

II. Write out three experiences when you have expressed your true loyalty to others.

III. Write out an experience when you have been betrayed and how it made you feel.

IV. Write out an experience when you betrayed someone and how you think your behavior affected this person.

CHAPTER 4

Sustained Through Humility and Contentment

I t is human nature to become prideful when we reach certain heights of status and achievement. Floating on top of the world, many who reach this plateau forget where they came from. Their egos take over and they begin to feel as though they themselves are the source of their prosperity. Consequently, their pride ultimately leads to self-destruction.

Success has a way of changing people. Money magnifies the character of a person. It gives people the ability to be more of who they truly are. Have you ever witnessed someone who seemed to be kind and pleasant, until they came up on a little good fortune? Then, their new found success rushed quickly to their heads, and they became very prideful and arrogant. This is a common problem for many who achieve success. If you do not learn to develop good character, you could also fall into this category.

In this chapter, we will examine the importance of humility and contentment. Through examples that will give us an up close look at various character flaws, you will learn the virtue of humility and contentment. Gaining these vital character traits are essential in developing good character. Do not take the information in the chapter lightly. Absorb it and apply it to your everyday life!

It's important to know God doesn't want us to be arrogant people. Those who are arrogant solely take credit for their own success. Our hardships allow us to see we do not have ultimate control over our destiny, only God does. We have the ability to make choices and God has the ultimate decision of granting us victory or failure. Without Him, we are nothing? He is the One who gives us the power to obtain success. It is God's desire that we look to Him for help. As we develop a relationship with God, and rely on Him for our provision, He will ultimately grant us prosperity!

Throughout this series we discussed how God wishes to be our Friend and our Partner. He desires to be first in our lives. We learned that God uses people as vehicles to bring us the necessary provisions we need. God doesn't want us to be reliant on people, places or things. Instead, He wants us to realize that He is our Source! God also wants us to recognize we need His help to sustain. When we become prideful, our actions tell God we don't need Him, and we can do things on our own. In this case, God detaches His flow of blessings to remind us that we are nothing without Him!

Many people have achieved awesome heights of fame and prestige, only to be dethroned. Imagine being nasty, prideful and disrespectful to others and then falling down from grace, and even possibly needing those whom you have crossed. That can be a terrible experience! People hate arrogant people! No one wants to be belittled or disrespected by someone else. When people suffer hard times who were once nasty to others, instead of receiving loving help, they are laughed at and ridiculed. We do not want that to be our fate! This time around, let's live life with integrity, so that we can enjoy long-term success and prosperity! Living this lifestyle requires humility.

It is a misconception that being humble is to be weak, or to let others mistreat you, or use you. Humility requires three main ingredients. To be humble is to be grateful for your achievements, to recognize the Source of your success (which is God), and to be open to change or correction. There is nothing wrong with feeling proud of your accomplishments, or taking pride in what you do. God's desire is for each of us to possess a good measure of self-esteem and confidence. The problem arises when we go overboard, believing we, in fact, are superior to others and powerful in our own strength.

When we reach our goals in life, we must make a concentrated effort to always maintain a level head. When good fortune comes, we are to thank God for His provisions, and maintain our normal code of ethics and behavioral patterns. Under no circumstances should we let success get to our heads, because it will block our provisions.

God will only give us what we are able to sustain. He rewards us according to our character. If God knows money will corrupt us and ultimately block us from achieving our purpose here on earth, He will only give us provision in the moderation that we are able to handle. If we want to receive blessings from God, we must prepare ourselves to be able to handle them! Our preparation begins with working on "self" and our character.

It is important that we never make people, places and things, or even accomplishments, our idols. We can enjoy them, but we are not to worship or serve them. It is a dangerous thing to build our lives centered around God's creations, putting them above the Creator Himself. When we make people, places or things our idols, God removes them to show us their true value. This can be a painful process! Life becomes more joyous when we realize material things are all replaceable. Whatever God gave you yesterday, He can give you again today!

Whatever we lose in life, we can also gain back. Therefore, it's important not to get caught up into the temporary pleasures of the world. When we are able to see that success and achievement by the world's standards are highly overrated, and they can be snatched at any time, it helps us to not put our trust in idols. Instead, we put our trust in God, who is the true Source of our provisions. If one door closes in our lives, God will open up another door. When we maintain this mentality it is easy to remain humble because we have a correct perception about the value of the provisions we are allotted.

Anything in life that has the ability to hurt you is considered an idol. At times, people may disappoint us, but they should never possess the power to devastate us, or take us off course. The same principle is true concerning material possessions. If we lose something, of course, we may be disappointed, but we should never be hurt to the point of total devastation. This kind of hurt lets us know the object or thing we worshiped had too much of a value in our eyes. Unconsciously, we made it an idol. An idol is anything or anyone whom we place before God. Be certain, God will always dethrone our idols! Whatever we have the ability to walk away from, we have mastered! When you are able to walk away from a thing, you are saying by your actions, "You don't control me, nor are you my source."

When we walk away from things that threatened our well-being or our quality of life, we are also saying to God, "I trust You to bring me new provisions; You are my Source, my Partner and my Friend." Having the proper perspective helps us to maintain humility.

When we become prideful, we generally become boastful, too! We look down on people who do not have the same things we have. Secretly, and even outwardly, we begin to believe we are better than others. As a result, we treat people badly to sustain our own false sense of esteem. Arrogant people worship themselves and their accomplishments. They believe they have made it because of what they have obtained. They make a flashy display to others of what they have in order to maintain their false sense of esteem. In their minds, they will never fall because they believe that they are too good for anything bad to happen to them.

Arrogance is recognized in a person's communication and interaction with others. They often praise themselves in their conversations and want people to recognize the depth of their success. Arrogant individuals are selfish. They are all about themselves. Whatever they do for others has a motive behind it. They give only to be recognized and praised. Additionally, when a person is arrogant, he or she will recognize the faults of others, but cannot see their own faults. These people belittle others to make themselves appear to be better. They live life worshipping "self," and they do whatever they can to bring themselves more glory.

Arrogance is the doorway to self-destruction. It blinds an individual from being able to recognize and change their true faults. The energy arrogance produces is powerful and very negative. It genuinely makes a person believe in their heart that he or she is superior to others and can accomplish anything. This energy causes them to haphazardly inflict pain on their prey. They justify their actions by believing their victims are beneath them, and deserve the pain inflicted. They also believe most people around them should cater to their needs and take part in their self-worship. Ultimately, arrogance leads a person to insanity, causing their decisions to be off balance and out of tune with their surroundings. This leads to self-destruction.

Humble people are able to embrace and maintain success, because they are always open to wisdom and correction. Humility says, "I don't know it all and I always have room to grow." It is the spirit that most people are glad to be around. Humility is open and inviting. It shares what it has with others and is always willing to accept more help. It has a heart that admits when it is wrong, and learns from past mistakes.

Humility doesn't allow one to get mad at constructive criticism. It enables a person to listen before he or she speaks and gladly accept a helping hand. Humility makes us wise and acknowledges our Source of provision. Even when we obtain prestige or accomplishments, we remain on a steady course. Humble people do not let success get the best of them. Instead, they acknowledge God and continue striving to achieve their purpose on earth.

One of the major character flaws within human nature is stubbornness. People desire to be free spirits, who wish to do whatever they please. Many hate to be corrected or advised by others. Instead of embracing wise counsel, they despise it! Stubborn people do not listen to anyone except themselves. Deep in their hearts they believe they know everything! They never see themselves as being the problem. Instead, everything is always someone else's fault. Stubborn people become locked in their own illusions. They actually believe their way is right. Consequently, they remain stagnated and unable to grow.

Many of us were warned by several people to change our ways before imprisonment. Our stubborn nature overrode the suggestions and constructive criticism of others. Instead of listening, we disobeyed and took our own course in life. Consequently, we stand in the dilemma we are stuck in today, imprisonment. Had we only listened and did something about ourselves and our behavior we could have prevented our mishaps. This time around life must be different! Instead of feeling like others are badgering us, let's listen to their advice. Take the good points and throw away the bad. By doing so, we can learn a lot and avoid unnecessary hardships.

Breaking the habit of stubbornness takes time, hard work and diligence. We must train ourselves to be open minded and accept the fact that we don't know it all. In order to become wise, we must be willing to learn. Willingness is determined by our behavior. The old saying is, "When the student is ready, the teacher will appear," is true. No one delights in teaching a stubborn student. When we open our hearts to change and are willing to listen to others, we open the doors for help to come our way. No matter what level of achievement we receive in life, we can always learn more from someone else. A wise person keeps their heart and mind open to learn from others, no matter how much they already know!

If we want to be successful, we must rid ourselves of stubbornness and recognize God as our Source. In addition, we must admit we do not know it all, nor do we have all the solutions. Therefore, we must open our hearts to receive help from others in times of need and be grateful for those who lend us a helping hand. Maturity and advancement come when we rid ourselves of stubbornness!

Humble people are content with who they are. They understand the key to successful living is always working on "self." Instead of being envious and jealous of others, they are caught up into fixing "self." They recognize promotion is based on their ability to sustain it, while also recognizing that God is their Source. Instead of hating on the success of others, humble people cheer others on while continuing to work on "self." They understand with hard work and diligence, they, too, can one day soar to great levels of achievement.

Humble people are not afraid to share what they know or what they have with others. They understand the Universal Law of Reciprocity: "The more you give is the more you receive." Therefore, humble people seek opportunities to share their gifts and help empower others to achieve their best. These people delight in seeing the success of others around them, because it is simply their nature!

Humble people realize in certain seasons they must do without and make sacrifices in life to get where they want to go. In these seasons, they become content with what they have, knowing that their hardships are only temporary and the best is yet to come. Humble people don't mind stepping down to permanently step back up. They don't concern themselves with what others may say or think about them. Instead, they keep their eyes on the prize and take the correct path to achieve success. Humble people know all short cuts lead to the path of destruction, so they plan their course accordingly.

For those of us who are incarcerated, many of us have grown accustomed to certain things and have gained a certain status or image we feel we must live up to. Secretly, our worst fear is to hear someone say, "Girl, she fell off!" To spare ourselves the embarrassment, we do whatever we have to do to sustain the praise and attention of people. This pattern is SELF DESTRUCTIVE!

If we want to achieve long-term success, we have to understand we must first make a sacrifice. We have learned from past dilemmas that "rocket ship" success is always temporary. What good is it to shoot to the top, only to come crashing back down? Instead of building our house on faulty sticks, let's build it on bricks!

Many of us are coming home from prison to absolutely nothing. We have lost all the things we obtained in the past.

Deep down inside, we are nervous about going back out to the free world. We have no clue how we will be able to acquire the material things we need to start over. As a result, our pride and arrogance may very well get the best of us, and lead us back down the path to destruction. This does not have to be our fate! We can program our minds to be ready to step down, in order to step back up permanently.

There are many public assistance programs and grants available to ex-felons coming home from prison. Each of us has the option to go back to school, or to obtain a skill that the state or government will assist us with paying for. This may mean struggling for a little bit of time until we get back on our feet, but the results are well worth it! If we establish ourselves the correct way, we no longer have to worry about losing the things we obtain. This time, when we reach the top, we will sustain our success!

One of the most destructive character flaws one can have is to be jealous and envious of others. Jealousy is a deadly poison that eats away at our hearts, causing us to be angry, bitter and vicious. Jealous people focus their energy on tearing down others rather than improving "self." Jealousy is a seed that quickly grows. It may at first appear harmless, yet it swiftly turns into an uncontainable monster. Jealous people are very negative and critical to others. You can recognize them by their conversation and their actions. These people live to speak badly or complain about others. Everything they do is centered around pulling people down in order to make themselves appear to be better.

Jealous people are dangerous! They will secretly destroy you, step on you, or rob you, by any means necessary! These people are destructive to themselves as well as others. They are not content with themselves. Because they dislike their image they want others to dislike their own images too. It's like the old saying, "Misery loves company."

Jealous people can be detected by their words and actions. If you have some sort of good fortune, and you share it with them, they will not join in on your victory. Instead, the jealous person will always find some sort of fault with what you have done. In addition, they wait for you to make an error, which they will quickly pick up on. Then, they will beat you down with criticism. They intentionally criticize others who they feel have achieved more than them. It is hard for jealous people to acknowledge the success of anyone except themselves. Instead, they look for the bad in everyone and wait for the opportunity to expose it. Jealous people are dangerous as they attempt to get others to join in on their lynching parties. Therefore, when you come in contact with jealous people, do your best to get away from them! Even if they don't attack you at first, yet constantly attack others, beware you will be next on their list!

If you are a jealous person, you must work hard on getting rid of this negative trait! Do your best to work on improving "self," and take your attention off of others. Learn to be content with what you have and who you are. Instead of being jealous of others, seek God to give you the things you desire. As you become happy with "self," God will bless you with more. On the other hand, if you remain jealous and envious of others you will block your own blessings; this will keep you stagnated in life. The only way to be successful is to become grateful for who you are, and rid yourself of jealously.

Now that we understand the principle of humility and contentment, as well as the detriments of stubbornness and jealousy, let's take a look at some real life examples that illuminate these character traits.

EXAMPLE

Anna Lee Jones and Thomas Jones had three sons they worked hard to raise in Indianapolis, Indiana. The Joneses were a very religious family; the parents prayed earnestly for the success of their three boys, Junior, Roger and Earl.

Junior graduated high school and went away to college. His goal was to be a doctor, so he worked hard to pay his way through school.

Roger had a great talent of playing basketball, and he went directly to the NBA from high school.

Earl was the youngest child who was often spoiled by his parents and his brothers. Earl didn't like school so he dropped out and hung out in the neighborhood instead.

When Roger made it to the NBA, life changed for his entire family. He moved the family to Chicago where Junior was going to college and bought a big house for the family to live in.

Earl kicked back and enjoyed the new-found riches of his brother. He cruised the streets in the brand new Cadillac Escalade Roger bought him. On the other hand, Junior remained in school. Instead of accepting lavish gifts from his brother, he accepted money and put it into a savings account for his future.

Life went well for the Joneses. Roger was on major billboards, magazines, and television. Many began to praise Roger's talent to play basketball. As a result, newfound fortune and success went straight to Roger's head. He began to believe he was superior to everyone and treated people harshly, including his parents.

When Roger got mad at his family for not showing him enough praise and attention, he would gain control by stopping the checks he sent to pay the bills. When his mother scolded him about his actions, Roger even cut off her credit card account. One day Mrs. Jones went to the grocery store to buy food and was embarrassed when her credit card declined. Roger became an egotistical monster. Life was all about him. Junior didn't like his brother's actions. He decided to work while going to school to make sure his parents always had their own money, so they wouldn't have to depend on Roger.

Earl became Roger's shadow. He traveled the country with Roger and enjoyed the gifts Roger gave him for his praise. Earl loved his new life, so he kept his true feelings about Roger to himself. Instead of getting on Roger about his bad behavior, Earl would find others to criticize and put down. Earl and Roger spent most of their time together talking about people they felt were less superior than them.

In a game against the Lakers, Roger decided it was time to embarrass Colby Bryant, the team's top player, attempting to call him out on the court. Roger was extremely confident his skill set exceeded Colby Bryant's so this particular night he made up his mind he would showcase his talent for the world. During the second half of the game he made a move to dunk on Colby and broke his right leg. Roger was rushed to the hospital and it was determined he would never be able to play basketball again.

Shattered and depressed, Roger moved back home. He was laughed at and ridiculed by his friends, whom he had abandoned in the height of his fame. It seemed like no one gave Roger any support, not even Earl. Instead of Earl having Roger's back as he expected, Earl began to put Roger down, telling him how much he really despised his ways. This hurt Roger more than anything!

Shortly after Roger's injury, Junior finished school and became a prestigious doctor in Chicago. He paid off the family *home and even helped Roger get back on his feet. Junior's compassion had a major effect on Roger. It made him realize the severity of his arrogance, and Roger repented to God for his bad behavior. This enabled Roger to take back control of his life and turn his adversity around. Today, he is the coach of a well-known college team. He has a wife and two kids and makes good money.*

Roger does his best to always stay humble. As a result, Roger has many good friends. Today, he recognizes success can be temporary, so he values what counts, which is his relationship with God and his family. Junior and Roger are best friends. They often hang out together in their spare time.

On the other hand, Earl still stays at home with his family. He never recovered from the fact his lavish lifestyle was taken away. He still blames Roger for his mishaps. Instead of trying to improve his life, Earl hangs out with his homies at the corner store and he sells marijuana on the side to sustain his lifestyle. The height of his day is making jokes about people who walk by.

The example of the three brothers gives us an up close view of the life of the humble, the arrogant and the jealous. After reading this story, which of these traits do you think you possess?

It is important to analyze ourselves honestly and make the necessary changes and correct our character flaws, so we can obtain and sustain a good life.

Are you ready to pick up the character traits of humility and contentment, and experience their benefits? If so, follow me in this short prayer: *"God, thank You for showing me the importance of humility and contentment. I now ask that You help me in my pursuit to humility. Give me a heart that is pure and pleasing unto You. Help me to always remember the Source of my blessings and teach me how to be content with myself. Erase all traits of envy and jealousy from within me. Give me the strength to always be happy with the achievement of others and the willingness to help others achieve success. Open my heart to always be willing to learn and to accept constructive criticism. I thank You for transforming my heart. I now receive my new heart of humility and contentment. Amen."*

Congratulations! You have *made* another huge step in your pursuit to a greater "self." Humility and contentment will take you a long way in life! Honor this character trait and it will in turn honor you! God bless.

QUESTIONS

1) What is humility?
2) What is arrogance?
3) Why is being prideful and arrogant dangerous?
4) What does it mean to be stubborn?
5) Why is being stubborn harmful?
6) What are the dangers of jealousy and envy?
7) How can you easily identify jealous people?

WRITING ASSIGNMENT

Write out an affirmation of the steps you can take to always remain humble, and to be content with who you are and with what you have.

CHAPTER 5

Generosity That Provokes Prosperity

I t is human nature to move about life simply caring for our own needs. The common belief is: the more that we get, the more we should hoard for ourselves. As a result, life becomes a pursuit to gain as much as we can. Instead of honoring and helping our neighbors, we step on them, or over them, in pursuit of our own goals. Consequently, life becomes self-centered and off balance, as our focus becomes the chase to receive self-satisfaction.

When our objective is to hoard our riches, it makes it very difficult to depart with what we have. We falsely believe whatever we give to someone else will take away from what we should have. Therefore, we become hoarders who refuse to lend those in need of a helping hand. This mentality is not pleasing to God. It is dangerous behavior that will ultimately lead to self-destruction!

God put each of us on this planet to perform a certain task. That task is called our purpose. Our purpose is always centered around giving something of value to others that God has given to us. It can include our time, our money, our talent or our service. When we refuse to be generous to others, it is impossible to obtain true fulfillment. As a result, our motives become contaminated and we block our provision from God, because we are defying His principles.

In this chapter, we will discuss the importance of generosity and the detriment of being selfish. We will also take a look at common every-day examples of generosity and selfishness to illuminate the principles we learn. Generosity is an important characteristic we need to develop to obtain and sustain a good life. Therefore, take the principles in this chapter seriously and implement them into your everyday living!

Generosity is the act of giving to, or helping others, without any hidden motives or objectives. When we are generous to others, we honor God with our service. Our acts of generosity aren't performed to please man; they are done to honor the Creator by fulfilling His purpose for us on earth. In essence, when we are generous to others, we are offering God our service.

Giving to others should never be based on what we can get back in return. We give to others because we know it is the right thing to do. When we give our service with expectancy of something in return, that is not considered an act of generosity. In that instance, our service is actually considered lending and bartering. We must always check our motives when we give to others. We do this by asking these questions: Am I expecting anything in return? And, how do I feel about departing with my gift? As we ask ourselves these questions, we are able to analyze our intents and properly align our hearts to give with the right spirit.

There are four main gifts we can give to others. They include our time, our money, our talent, and our service.

We give our time to others when we talk and listen to those in need of comfort and friendship. We give our money as a monetary gift, or we utilize our money to purchase a gift for those in need. We use our talents to help uplift someone who is in need. We give our service when we volunteer our time in a group effort, or individually, to encourage, help and uplift those in need. All acts of generosity are a part of working in our purpose.

We are called to give back to others what God has given to us. The universal law of reciprocity says, "The more that we give is the more that we will receive." That means the more we distribute into the universe, the more we can expect to come back to us. The key to understanding this principle is recognizing Whom we should expect to receive from—our Creator. Our expectancy or provision should be sought only from God. He is our Provider, not man! When our expectancy is in God, instead of man, people cannot easily disappoint us. When we give to others with no expectancy from them, if they are ungrateful or do not reciprocate the gesture we are not affected. What we did was an act of service to God, out of the kindness of our hearts. As a result, we are pleased with ourselves regardless of how the recipient acts or feels towards us.

When we are generous to others, we are successfully walking in our purpose by giving our service to God, so we can expect an abundant harvest in return. God takes pleasure in giving and entrusting us with His gifts, when He knows we will properly distribute them. God entrusts us with gifts so we can become vessels who distribute them to others. The more that we give, the more He will in turn give to us!

Look at the world's richest people, such as Bill Gates and Oprah Winfrey; they are huge givers! These individuals donate millions of dollars to help others, looking for nothing in return. They already have success fame and fortune, yet they continue to give. God is happy with their sincere efforts, so He continues to bless them even more. These people are walking in their purpose, which allows God to use them as distributors who funnel gifts to those in need.

Can God trust you to share the blessings He entrusts you with? The greater relationship you gain with God and the more He can trust you, the more you will have. When you hoard the things you have, your actions say to God, "I don't trust You to give me more. Therefore, I will take care of myself." This action will block your blessing flow. When God can't trust you to perform your God-given duties on earth, He limits your provision! Are you stopping up your blessing flow? If so, remove the blockage today and learn to give with a pure heart!

Selfish people are self-centered. All they care about is their own gain. Selfishness deteriorates our hearts and turns our focus off of God and onto our own self-agenda. When our focus is off, our lives become out of balance. In addition, our thinking and our actions are adversely affected. Consequently, we become predators, rather than lovers of people, and our motives cause us to miss the mark of our purpose.

When we are selfish to others, the law of attraction causes others to also be selfish to us. We were put on this world to be a part of God's family. God has skillfully equipped each of us with unique skill sets and abilities. Some of us operate as the arms and hands of God's body, while others operate as the legs and feet. We all have different assignments, yet we each have a purpose to perform specific duties that will help the greater good. We need each other to survive! When we are selfish we block the help of others from assisting us.

God has people who are assigned to us that are waiting for us to get in alignment with purpose, so that they can receive our help. We can't assist people if our motives are incorrect. Our sincerity will be determined by our actions. If our actions are not genuine, our recipients will quickly know by our attitude and our performance. When we do things with the wrong motives our gifts do not have the powerful effect they should. In addition, God does not reward us when we give with wrong intentions.

God's desire is that we give with a heart of joy. When we give a person a gift it should be done just as if God came down from Heaven and gave it to the recipient Himself. When our motives are pure, our gifts are given to others with care and compassion. Genuine care and compassion have the power to invoke change in the hearts of others. Then, our love and generosity become contagious. That person will want to bless someone else, just as we blessed them. This sparks a powerful cycle of love and generosity, which has the ability to pierce the hearts of others. Just like many of us, a lot of people have been beat down and battered by life. When they witness others who are genuinely good to them, with no hidden motives or agendas, it brings inner joy and sparks life back into the recipient. Generosity can be life changing! We have the power to heal a wounded soul simply by our acts of generosity and love.

When we give to others, it should be done gracefully and in moderation. We are called to give to those who are less fortunate, not to those who are lazy and unwilling to do for themselves. Our gifts should be what people need, not necessarily what they want. We are not to disable people by giving or doing things for those who can do for themselves. Disabling others is not an act of generosity. By disabling a person, you actually hurt them more than you help them. Therefore, think about your actions before you perform them, even your giving. Make sure you are being a blessing and not a hindrance.

Throughout this series, we have been working intensely to find our purpose in life, which is the assignment we were put on this earth to do. We have worked on assessing our skill sets and talents and have discovered our inner strengths that can help others. It is the process of discovering purpose that helps illuminate the power of generosity. As we operate in the area of gifting we were purposed to do, we uplift and strengthen others and at the same time receive self-fulfillment. We learned that the inner void we all have inside cannot be fulfilled by people, places and things. Happiness and fulfillment are not truly obtained until we learn how to walk in our purpose. Generosity is a large part of fulfilling purpose.

As we take our minds off of our self-interest and put it into the help and service of others, God then rewards us through His provisions and He provides us with inner joy. The inner joy God gives is unlike anything a human, or any other creation, can provoke. Walking in purpose allows us to feel good about "self" and motivates us to want to soar in life. Purpose becomes our protection from evil and self-destruction. It gives us the strength and joy we need to overcome life's dilemmas. Therefore, finding our purpose is true fulfillment and the reason we all were put on this earth!

Many of us are experiencing a rough time in life. This season of imprisonment may be one of the toughest experiences we have had to encounter. In prison, everyone tries to take care of their own self-interest in order to survive this stormy season of life. Prisoners are generally bitter about their circumstances and care only about survival. This selfish behavior only amplifies our problems even more.

If we spend our time of incarceration only focusing on "self," we leave our minds open to constantly replay our mishaps. In turn, we become sad and depressed about all we have had to endure. Consequently, we developed a "woe is me" mentality. This can be self-destructive and make imprisonment even harder to endure.

When we stop solely focusing on "self" and begin to help others around us, we are able to recognize our dilemmas aren't as bad as we may have thought. There is always someone else who is experiencing more severe hardships than we are. When we recognize our blessings and the things we have to be grateful for, it helps take our minds off of what we temporarily do not have.

Instead of worrying about what we don't have, let's get caught up into what we do have, and how we can help others to overcome their dilemmas. As we focus on helping and giving to others, God in turn will provide for us. Suddenly, what we were lacking will mysteriously appear! Someone will give us the very thing we were missing. It is our actions that begin a cycle of generosity which allows us to also become the recipients of help.

The only way to open the door of prosperity is to take the first step and begin to give. As we become generous, the doors of the universe open to us, and we begin to reap our harvest. Our actions bring us into closer alignment with our Creator, who in turn rewards us for our service to Him. Prosperity starts when we learn to give out of a pure heart, with no hidden motives or strings attached.

Now that we know the importance of generosity and giving with the correct heart, let's explore the gifts of "self" and how we can give, even while imprisoned.

Generosity does not just consist of giving our money. Money at times can be impersonal and not help the situation. When we give the gift of "self," which is giving our time, our service or our talent to others, it can have a tremendous effect! What gift of "self" can you give today to help someone else in need?

When we learn skills and obtain knowledge God does not intend for us to keep the information we learn to ourselves; He desires us to share what we know with others. God delights in our sharing. Knowledge brings enlightenment. It is the key ingredient that helps people to solve problems. As we share the skill sets we learn with others, it reinforces what we already know, while helping empower someone else. The old saying "We teach it, to keep it," is true! The more we share the knowledge we obtain, the stronger it becomes imbedded within us! Who can you share the information you have learned in the *Voices of Consequences Enrichment Serie*s with? The more you empower others, the more doors that will be open to you!

The gift of time can be an awesome present. We can give the gift of time by sitting down and listening to others and sharing our positive feedback and past experiences. This is also called the gift of encouragement. By giving others our time, we open the doors for someone else to be there for us when we are in need. Giving our gift of time does not include gossiping or talking negatively about others. It is lending your ear of support and letting the recipient know they are not alone. What words of encouragement can you help someone with? Your words can have a grand effect on the lives of others, and change and inspire people in ways you never dreamed or imagined! Will you allow God to use you by giving someone the gift of encouragement today?

Our gifts can also include giving something of monetary value to another. Many of us are blessed to have an abundance of material items. It is a blessing to be a blessing. What do you have that you can give that may help someone else out? Don't hoard the things you own. Hoarding only slows down the blessing flow! When you have enough, or extra, consider giving to someone else in need. By giving, you open the doorway for God to give you even more!

Even though we are in prison, we can still be a blessing to others. Sit and think about the ways you can honor God by giving to others right where you are. Make sure your heart and your intentions are pure. Give in the same manner God has given to you! As you make generosity a habit, you will experience the doorways of prosperity flooding open in your life!

Now that we understand the ways we can give, and how we can give the gift of "self," let's explore some everyday examples of generosity so we can increase our knowledge of giving.

EXAMPLE 1 - THE GIFT OF TIME

Alicia is a nurse at a major hospital. She has genuine compassion and concern for hurting people, so she loves her job! She cares for each of her patients as she would want someone to care for her. As a result, she quickly advanced in her position, and all the patients she cares for love her.

Alicia gets paid to do her job, but she felt as though she wanted to provide more services without receiving any compensation. As a result, she decided to give back twenty minutes out of her one-hour lunch break each day, to spend time with her patients.

Alicia goes to different hospital room during her lunch hour and brings the patients newspapers, magazines and puzzles. She talks to them about how they feel, their family life, and events going on in the world. As Alicia listens to the patients and gives her support, they each feel the genuine compassion she has in her heart. It is no surprise why Alicia has been constantly voted "nurse of the month" for several months in a row! Her kindness, generosity and acts of love are second to none!

Example 2 - The Gift of Talent and Skill Set

Roger is a teacher at a local school in Orlando, Florida. Roger loves to teach. As a little boy, he dreamed of becoming a teacher and worked hard to accomplish his goal.

Roger was glad to get his license after completing college, so he could finally start teaching. He spent several hours working with the students in his school to help increase the school's poor testing average on statewide examinations.

Roger's passion enabled him to discover a system that worked in helping to improve his student's test scores. Eager to see the whole school advance, just as his students did, Roger volunteered his services and created an after school program. He volunteered every day for two hours after school. As a result, after only seven months, the entire school's scores increased drastically.

The Superintendent of Schools was so impressed by Roger's act of kindness and his gift of time that Roger was promoted to become a principal after only two years of service.

Even until this day, Roger takes education and the advancement of his students very seriously. He still volunteers at his state renowned latchkey, after school program. The program he created is now a model that other principals follow in the surrounding areas. Roger's success would not be possible without his gift of time.

Example 3 - The Gift of Service

Kanika was a Federal prisoner at Danbury Correctional Federal Institution, where she was serving an 80-month sentence for bank fraud.

Kanika was disheartened about her incarceration, because she believed her lengthy sentence was unjust. Kanika spent several hours in the law library researching ways she could reduce her sentence.

One day during her research she came across 2B1.1 in the Federal Sentencing Guidelines and discovered an error in her loss amount calculation.

One of the law clerks helped Kanika prepare a 2255 motion to go before the courts to reduce her sentence. Kanika became intrigued with the law after discovering the loophole in her case and decided to help other women in Danbury do the same kind of research on their cases.

Faithfully, Kanika volunteered her service to other women who needed her help. Waiting for her own decision from the courts, Kanika witnessed three other girls get sentence reductions for their cases, based upon her help.

One day Kanika was called to her counselor's office where she received the legal mail. To her dismay, the courts had denied Kanika's motion to lessen her sentence. Kanika was deeply disappointed, but something inside wouldn't allow her to give up. She continued volunteering her legal services, helping other women prepare their court motions and briefs. One day, while offering her gift of service to another inmate, Kanika came across a law she felt could reverse her own case.

Once again, Kanika prepared her motion and prayed to God that it would be heard and approved. As Kanika awaited her answer, she continued giving her service of legal assistance, and several more women benefited from it! Four inmates were released from prison and Kanika became highly sought after because of her knowledge of the law.

One day over the loud speaker, Kanika was called to R&D. She was granted an immediate release and told to pack her things and go! All of the girls were excited, but Kanika still had work she was doing for several of the women. Kanika left prison and stayed true to her word. She finished all the legal work she started in prison at home.

Today, Kanika owns her own paralegal research company. She has helped dozens of prisoners reduce and vacate their sentences. Kanika takes joy in what she does. She knows how it feels to be locked up and in need of the assistance of others. Kanika's compassion, love and care for prisoners allows her to soar as she walks in her God-given purpose!

EXAMPLE 4 - THE GIFT OF MONEY

Cynthia was sentenced to life in prison for being the ring leader of a prominent drug ring in Chicago. Cynthia was devastated about her sentence. She wanted to die, as she felt she would spend the rest of her life in prison.

For several years, Cynthia was very mean and bitter to others, especially those who had a short sentence. Inside, she resented them because they had another chance at life, which she didn't have. Consequently, Cynthia was very selfish. She would rarely ever share her things or her time with others. Cynthia was also known to be heartless and rude.

One day, Cynthia met Kim who was a bright spirited girl from New York, serving a short sentence for mail fraud. Kim was drawn to Cynthia and always came around to check on her. At first, Cynthia was mean to Kim, but Kim's sincerity pierced Cynthia's heart and the two girls became friends.

Kim had no family, so she often went without the luxuries of others. Cynthia quickly saw Kim's misfortune and began to help her out with commissary. Kim was moved by Cynthia's generosity. As a result, she decided she was ready to change her life and move on to the right track of life.

Kim went home after her sentence ended, and to Cynthia's surprise, she stayed in touch. Kim sent Cynthia cards, letters and pictures on a regular basis, which brought Cynthia great joy.

Kim started working as a receptionist at a law firm back in her home town of New York City, where she met and married the senior partner of the firm. Kim brought Cynthia's case to her husband's attention, and he decided to take her case on Pro Bono.

By the grace of God, Kim's husband was able to find the loophole that overturned Cynthia's conviction! Cynthia was then able to take a plea for fifteen-years prison term, after her life sentence was vacated. Today, Cynthia has two years left in prison and has gained her hope back! The doors of prosperity opened for Cynthia with her act of generosity.

Are you ready to embrace the character trait of generosity and allow it to open doors of provision in your life?

If so, follow me in this short prayer: *"God, I thank You for showing me the importance of being generous. I now have the desire to take on the character trait of generosity as my own. Open my eyes and reveal to me opportunities to be generous to others. Clean my heart, rid me of all selfishness, and help me to always have clean pure motives in my giving. Bless me so I can be a blessing to others. Allow my gifts to pierce the hearts of my recipients, sparking change and joy deep down within them. Use me to start the cycle of generosity right where I am. Allow Your light to shine through me, so I can comfort others who are in need. I thank You now for divine direction and knowledge concerning my giving. My greatest desire is to please You in everything I do. I receive Your blessings and I take hold of the gift of generosity now. Amen."*

Congratulations! You have taken another huge step in your pursuit to a greater "self." You are now equipped with the gift of generosity. Utilize it to be a blessing to as many others as you possibly can. Today, you have positioned yourself to soar!

QUESTIONS

1) What is generosity?
2) In what four ways can you give to others the gift of "self?"
3) Why is giving important?
4) What is the Universal Law of Reciprocity?
5) What happens when we are selfish and refuse to give?
6) Is generosity an act of disabling others? Why or why not?

WRITING ASSIGNMENT

I. Write out three ways in which you can become more generous to others now. Take into account your skill sets, talents and abilities.

II. Write out three ways in which you can become more generous when you get out of prison. Take into account you future skill sets, talents and abilities as well as the skills you have now.

CHAPTER 6
The Strength of Joy and A Good Attitude

L ife is a series of obstacles and tests, which help us to grow and develop. Dilemmas are a part of the normal course of life; we will all encounter them at one time or another. It is human nature to feel as though everything should be good, all of the time. People do not like their normal course of life to be interrupted. Seldom do we enjoy change of any kind! When obstacles occur, they force us to change. If we wish to overcome them, we must stretch ourselves and grow. Obstacles require us to think and work diligently.

Human nature is to become comfortable with things as they are, so often we settle to avoid change. Obstacles force us to move to the next level or phase in life, whether we like to or not. Fear of the unknown makes many of us unsettled. Instead of embracing obstacles, we become bitter and disgruntled. We develop the, "why me?" syndrome and move about sluggishly with disappointment. This attitude steals our joy and our peace. In addition, it makes life miserable for ourselves and others around us.

The key to living an enjoyable life is to maintain our joy, regardless of what situation we may be experiencing. When we are in tune with "self," we develop the ability to tap into our inner joy, at any time we need it. Tapping into our inner joy gives us the strength we need to push forward and conquer every obstacle that comes our way! Joy is the fuel we need to sustain during life's difficulties. Without joy, life is miserable and it's difficult to succeed. We don't have to stay stuck in depression and disappointment any longer! We can overcome the depths of sorrow with the strength of our inner joy!

In this chapter, we will learn about the importance of maintaining our inner joy and how to tap into it at any time through the power of "self." This chapter contains key strategies and techniques. Learn them and make them a part of your daily habits. As you will see, the power of your inner joy has the ability to change your entire quality of life!

Our ability to enjoy life is based on our perception of how we view the events that occur. If our perception is wrong, we are subjected to living a distorted, miserable life. Joy begins when we are correctly able to view our circumstances and situations for what they truly are.

Throughout the *Voices of Consequences Enrichment Series*, we learned that we have the power to overcome any obstacles by changing our perception. We learned obstacles will always come, but we have acquired the skill set and ability to overcome them! Therefore, we no longer look at obstacles as a dilemma, which cannot be solved. Indeed, we now view them as opportunities to grow and advance.

Today, we no longer look for the bad; we consciously search for the good that can come out of every situation. We now ask ourselves the questions: "What will I learn from this experience? How can I utilize this situation as a stepping stone to advance? And, what is God trying to get me to see or recognize?"

When we answer these questions, we are able to see that there is a bigger, brighter picture! God doesn't send obstacles to kill us, or to beat us down. Obstacles are sent to strengthen us and to guide us into the next phase of life. They're the instruments God uses to help us grow!

When we understand the proper perspective of viewing life dilemmas, we remain calm and become strengthened to endure. Instead of being disappointed or complaining, we learn how to become grateful and rejoice in the midst of fiery storms. What we thought was a disappointment is actually an opportunity for promotion! We learned God only gives us provisions according to what we are able to handle. When we overcome our obstacles, we pass the test. Every test we pass comes with an equal reward!

Our pain and our struggles are never in vain. They help us to get in line with God's will and purpose for our lives. As we get in alignment with purpose, we pass the test, and the struggles we endure begin to cease. Therefore, when we encounter dilemmas and obstacles, we know it is God's way of saying, "It's time to work on 'self' and advance to the next level. I have something great in store for you, which I wish to give you. But, I have to make sure you are prepared to handle my blessings." God's gifts are perfect. They come with no sorrow. God will never give us what we are unable to sustain. Just as a parent will not give their eight-year old child a brand new car, God will not give us gifts that will destroy us.

Lack of knowledge has caused many of us to believe the things in life we endured were sent because God doesn't love us or because He is punishing us. In many cases, our views have been absolutely wrong! God chastens and disciplines those that He loves. He recognizes our potential, and He has a great purpose for each of us. Therefore, He utilizes obstacles to get us in alignment with His perfect plan. When we learn from our obstacles, make the necessary effort to change our ways, and get back on the right course, the reward that we are given is way greater than the pain we had to endure! When we are able to look back in the end, we will see it was all well worth it!

It is in the midst of our adversity that our character is developed, which causes our territory to become enlarged. In the midst of hardships, kings, queens and rulers are born! The best leaders in the world are those who have experienced hardships in life. Their experiences allow them to have genuine care and compassion for others. Instead of beating people down and misusing their authority, they uplift others. These leaders remember the pain that they too endured and comfort and compassion they were shown during their trials.

Right now, it may seem as if we are the underdogs and that everyone else has it better than we do, but the picture you see now is only temporary. We have gone through things in life that many could not endure. We have been dragged down and beaten by life's obstacles, yet, we are still standing strong! Others have used us and abused us, yet we still have the heart to forgive. Do not be misled! God sees, and knows all things! We have been tested and tried. Now it's time to become approved!

When we get that stamp of approval, we can go back into the free world on top! Remember, God always tests those whom He wishes to promote. Nothing is given without first passing the test. God wants to know what is in our hearts, and if we have the character to sustain the gifts He wishes to give us.

Knowing the purpose of trials and tribulations, we no longer become disappointed and angry when they arise. Instead, we look for the good in every situation. By doing so, we are able to sustain our joy!

Joy is the energy of strength and happiness that comes from within. Idols cannot bring us joy. It can only be derived from the passion within our hearts. Joy gives us the inner knowing that everything is going to be okay. It has power that is unimaginable, even the ability to take a broken heart and mend it back to health! Joy is the key ingredient we need to push us ahead in life. Just as a car needs fuel to drive, we need joy to move about vigorously.

Without joy, life is miserable! There is no peace in life without joy! When we do not have inner joy, depression and sadness overtake our beings, causing us to feel miserable and purposeless. This is the state that many people stay stuck in, which can lead to self-destruction or even suicide. It is dangerous to live life without joy!

Many of us have spent our entire lives searching for joy and happiness. We believed we could obtain it by seeking after false idols. Consequently, we have utilized all of our time and effort pursuing after what we thought would bring us joy, only to discover we were wrong! Some of us have even gone a step further in our pursuit. We believed we could find joy and happiness in drugs. Therefore, we got high and, at first, felt a great sensation that quickly slipped away. Then, we got high again and again, with efforts to try and sustain this sense of joy and peace. The very high we sought after, thinking it would sustain us, was the very thing that ended up resulting in our self-destruction.

Helpless and worn out, we all stand in the same place. Our hearts are empty and void and we are looking for fulfillment. Some of us, disillusioned to the truth, are still seeking fulfillment in the wrong places. Now that we are in prison with limited resources, many are seeking other women to fill our inner void. This, too, will result in disappointment!

We do not have to stay insane people, doing the same things, yet expecting different results! When you look outside of yourself for happiness it will only provide temporary relief, which will NEVER be sustained. What we have all been looking for has been within us the whole time! Inner joy brings true happiness and peace. Until we work within, we will always do without!

Inner joy comes when we change our perceptions and discover our true purpose. Instead of seeking people, places and things, and looking for provision within them, we now seek God who is our Provider. We know our "Higher Power" is our Partner and He always has our back! No matter what we go through, we know we are never alone. Our Partner will always defend and protect us! We know He only wants the best for us, so we are able to see His hand, even in the midst of our obstacles. When we have this assurance, we have the faith we need to make it! Our faith in our "Higher Power" brings us joy and strength within. As a result, when others are crying and complaining, we can laugh and rejoice. We know our dilemmas are only temporary. There is a prize to obtain at the end of the rainbow, so we pull up our sleeves and stand strong in the midst of adversity. We understand crying and complaining will only make our situations more difficult to endure, so we rid ourselves of all the heavy weights that attempt to hold us down. We keep our heads held high and we turn our faces to God. As our reward, our faith creates the inner joy we need to outlast our storm!

The only way to maintain our joy is to practice positive thinking. When fear, worry and doubt try to creep in, we must purposely change our thoughts. To overcome, we go into meditation and begin to think about the good that will come out of our challenges, rather than reflect on the bad. We flood our minds with positive thoughts of love, peace and joy. As a result, our bodies begin to feel the inner peace and joy we need to strengthen us.

Our feelings are our indicators. They alert us to the thoughts we are having. When we start to feel afraid or worried, we know that is because we have allowed ourselves to experience wrong thoughts. Instead of moping and allowing bad thoughts to overtake us, we must stop and reprogram our thinking by inputting positive thoughts into our minds. These positive thoughts change our course and allow us to be strengthened in the midst of adversity.

When fear, worry and doubt creep in, we now have the ability to go into prayer and meditation and seek our "Higher Power." We now know fear is: false evidence appearing real. It does not reveal our true reality, so we refuse to accept it! We overcome fear by meditating and communing with our "Higher Power." As we silently pray to Him during meditation, we envision ourselves being made whole through His power. In our minds, we see our problems passing away, and we experience the feelings of joy we will have when our hardships are over. We purpose our minds to see ourselves living the victorious life we desire. We make sure that picture is clear in our minds. We live in the house that we desire, we experience the comfort of our new friends and family, we work within our field of purpose, and we drive along the streets in the vehicle of our choice. As we experience freedom in our minds, we are making our prayer request to God. Our mental visualizations are saying to Him, "This is my desire. Will you please help make this experience my reality?"

The clearer you are able to envision your new life, the stronger your prayer petition becomes. Eventually, with hard work and diligence, your prayer request will indeed be answered. Soon it will become your reality!

It is human nature that when we experience difficulties we become bitter. As a result, we develop a bad attitude. This causes us to blame others for our own faults and treat innocent bystanders badly, due to our mishaps. This is not good! When we maintain a bad attitude, we radiate negative energy within the atmosphere causing more bad experiences to arise in our lives. When we are nasty to others, people are, in turn, nasty to us. This starts a negative cycle of adversity, which is motivated by our own negative behavior.

No matter what we experience in life, it is important to maintain a good attitude. Our outward expressions of joy permeate into the atmosphere, causing good things to come our way. When we are pleasant to people, we have the ability to positively affect them. Someone could be going through a difficult time, but our pleasant attitude can soothe them and spark joy into that person. In essence, when we maintain a good attitude, we give others our gift of joy. It is one of the most powerful gifts we can give! This gift is contagious and has the ability to spark life back into others.

It is human nature to interact with people in a similar fashion to the way they interact with us. As we know many are bitter and angry because of life's dilemmas, so they maintain a negative attitude. Just because people are negative to us doesn't mean we should be negative back to them. Two wrongs do not make a right! We overcome evil with good! By staying positive when others are negative to us, our kindness becomes a knife that pierces the hearts of our recipients. Eventually, they will see how awful their behavior is and our kindness will spark them to change. You get more from people with kindness than you do with anger or a bad attitude! When you are kind to those who wish to do you harm, their spirits will become convicted to change their wicked ways. It's not fun to fight with someone who doesn't join in the fight.

Remember the old saying, "It takes two to Tango?" Therefore, we have the ability to put out fires with our kindness. When people see you are unwilling to entertain their adverse behavior, they will move on to somebody else that will. We avoid negativity by refusing to join in it!

We must treat people the way we want to be treated. As we treat people well, we are sowing the seed for others to treat us well in return. It is important that we always check our attitude and be courteous at all times. As we become conscious of our behavior, we open the doors for joy to be obtained and sustained in our life. As we close the door to bad attitudes and negativity, we open the door to peace and prosperity.

When rough times come, refuse to allow yourself to become a victim. Instead, make up in your mind that you will be an overcomer! Refuse to grumble and complain. Purposely look for the good that is yet to come!

Another way to maintain your joy is to recount good memories and become thankful for what you have. When we become grateful for what we have, it takes our mind off of what we do not have. Become appreciative in the midst of adversity; it gives us the accelerated strength we need to get through the moment. When you recognize yourself becoming disgruntled, take control and stop yourself! Purposely think of all the things you are grateful for. As you do, you will feel inner peace that will enable you to maintain your joy!

Instead of mourning, discover ways you can have fun in your current season. Purposely find enjoyable activates to do while you are awaiting your breakthrough. Refuse to allow depression and sadness to settle in! Become active and utilize your time wisely. Find something fun and productive to do. As you get caught up into productive activities, your time will fly by! When we sit around and mope about life, time takes forever to go by. Therefore, take control and use your time wisely! The worst thing you can do while experiencing hardships is to pick up the company of negative people. Words are powerful containers that can harm us! If you sit around and allow negative people to inflict you with their words of discouragement, they will rob you of your joy, which will ultimately steal your peace. Therefore, refuse to let others put their trash into your can! Avoid negative people at all costs! Their energy is contagious and has the ability to keep you stagnant, which will have you feeling even worse than you were before they arrived.

Protect yourself by only surrounding yourself with positive people. If those you are around do not support you and encourage you when you are down, quickly rid yourself of them. Our joy is maintained when we surround ourselves with positive energy. Keep positive thoughts in your mind and surround yourself with positive people!

Now that we understand the strength and the importance of maintaining our joy and having a good attitude, let's take a good look at some up close examples that illustrate these character traits.

EXAMPLE 1 -

Dr. Schwartz had an office in Kansas City, Missouri. In July of 2002, he diagnosed two patients with cancer. Janice was diagnosed with breast cancer and William was diagnosed with lung cancer.

Both patients were heartbroken to get the disturbing news. Janice went home and put the sheets over her head, and she went into a deep depression. She constantly woke up in the middle of the night, suffering from panic attacks. Janice felt her life was over. As fear, worry and doubt took a hold over her, she quit work and sat home to await the bad fate she was told would occur.

On the other hand, William's illness sparked an inner desire to live life to the fullest. He began to travel and he regained a relationship with his "Higher Power." William refused to just give up. He sought Dr. Schwartz's assistance in figuring out what to do to overcome his dilemma. William decided to take chemotherapy treatments as a possible solution.

Janice also sought medical help from Dr. Schwartz, but she had little faith that the treatment would work. Janice kept repeating in her mind thoughts of misery and death. She often told people she was about to die and to enjoy the last of the times they had together.

In January of 2003, Janice died. When an autopsy was performed on her it was discovered that her death was caused by a heart attack and her alleged breast cancer wasn't cancer at all. The tumor in her breast was tested and found not to have any traces of cancer. Janice died as a result of a high level of stress. Fear, worry and doubt ultimately killed her!

On the other hand, William maintained his health. Each day he fed himself with positive thoughts through meditation. He began caring for "self," while he enjoyed his time with his family.

In August 2003, William was re-diagnosed as cancer free. He was able to overcome his obstacle by maintaining his faith and his joy throughout his dilemma.

Today, William lives a joyous life with his wife and his kids. He has a new outlook and cherishes his second chance at life. He is very close to his wife and his children. He always keeps in mind the things in life that count the most!

EXAMPLE 2 -

Charlotte worked at a bread factory for over ten years. She was the supervisor over production in the factory. Charlotte was advanced in age and wanted to become the chief operator over the factory, which would allow her to be more laid back in a corporate environment. Charlotte knew all the ins and outs of the factory operation, but her boss was a male chauvinist, who didn't feel that women should have high positions in the workplace.

Instead of promoting Charlotte, he had her train a young male factory worker whom he promoted over her. Charlotte was devastated and ready to quit. She couldn't believe she would have to answer to the young boy she trained who was clearly inexperienced.

Charlotte decided to stay at her job, even though she hated what was done to her. She forced herself to maintain a good attitude and she even helped out her new boss, who knew very little about the factory. She continued to smile and be nice to the owner of the company, which took him by surprise. He was sure Charlotte would be angry and bitter, because he knew what he did wrong.

The young boy ended up getting sick and Charlotte picked up his slack. She got to work two hours early each day and left two hours later to perform her normal duties, along with the duties of her boss. The owner was amazed to see how efficient Charlotte was at the duties she performed. He clearly saw by her work ethic, that Charlotte was faithful and committed to the bread factory.

The young boy returned to the factory and business resumed back to normal. One morning Charlotte came to work and greeted the owner with a smile, and he no longer could resist. The owner invited Charlotte into the office and apologized about how he neglected to promote her after all her years of service. He gave Charlotte a bonus and offered her the position as overseer of his entire organization, which included three other factories.

Today, the company is soaring! Charlotte teaches her staff to always maintain a good attitude and to work together in unity. As a result of Charlotte's efforts, the factory's production is at an all-time high! She is now vested in the company and owns shares in the corporation. It was Charlotte's good attitude that opened the door for her to be victorious in the end!

Are you ready to become victorious too, just like Charlotte? You can do so by overcoming your current dilemmas by increasing your inner joy and maintaining a good attitude. If you are ready to take on these positive character traits, follow me in this short prayer:

"God, I thank You for showing me the importance of maintaining my joy and having a good attitude. Regardless of what I go through, give me the ability to tap into my inner joy. Help me change my perspective, so that I will always look for the good in every circumstance and situation. Give me the divine insight to get to know 'self.' Show me the techniques that work for me, so that I can always maintain my joy. Give me a heart of gratitude that remains grateful for the things I have. Help me to appreciate and concentrate on my blessing, and help me to maintain a positive attitude throughout every situation I experience. Allow my expression to others to become a reflection of Your divine light that shines from within me. Please give my inner joy the power to pierce hearts of others, so they too can share in the gift of joy! I thank You for guidance and empowerment. I now receive Your joy within my heart. Amen."

QUESTIONS
1) What is joy!
2) Why is maintaining joy important?
3) Where does joy come from and how is it produced?
4) What are some techniques we can use to increase our joy?
5) Why is having a good attitude essential?
6) What is the detriment of letting discouragement and depression sink in?

WRITING ASSIGNMENT
Write out an acclamation of ways you can maintain your joy daily. Keep this acclamation close to you and read it each day. As you implement these techniques in your life, watch how you will soar and sustain your joy!

CHAPTER 7

The Virtue of Being Trustworthy and Dependable

We live in a society where broken promises have become the norm. People make commitments to others, without first counting the cost. As a result, words are used loosely without thought of how they may affect others. Our motives are geared toward our own advancement, so we say what we must to get what we need at the time. Many commit to jobs, financial obligations, organizations, family members, friends and even God, with no real intentions to perform our obligations. Consequently, our commitments and duties are left for others to pick up our slack, our reputations are ruined, and our words become baseless and void.

Life, for many of us, has spiraled out of control. In relationships, we have burned bridges we've once crossed. Now, in our attempt to return home, we have limited support to help get us where we need to go. Life has become a constant cycle of using and abusing others, including those who have our best interest at heart. As a result, due to our betrayal and lack of dependability, we have torn and broken many hearts. Therefore, those who truly love us, want to believe our words when we say, "This time life will be different. I promise, I'm going to do the right thing!" Unfortunately, experience has taught them that our words are not to be trusted. In their hearts, they truly want us to change. But, deep down inside, they don't know if change for us will ever be possible!

In this chapter, we will explore the virtue of being trustworthy and dependable to ourselves and to others. We will take an up close view of the effects of betrayal and lack of dependability. The objective of this chapter is to allow us to get a mirror view of our actions, their importance, and how they significantly affect others. This view will allow each of us to obtain the correct perspective about the virtue of being trustworthy and dependable, sparking change in our hearts and causing each of us to embrace these essential character traits.

Throughout the *Voices of Consequences Enrichment Series*, we have discussed the fact that we all are a part of God's wonderful family. We were each designed to perform a specific set of duties here on earth, which is called our purpose. Everyone is unique, and designed to perform individual tasks. In essence, we are all different parts of God's body here on earth. Some of us operate as the hands and arms, and others perform as the legs and feet. Each part is different; yet the arms need the feet to operate, just as the hands need the legs to properly function. Understanding this concept, we know that in order to perform in perfect union, as God has intended us to, we need each other!

When we are not trustworthy, or dependable to ourselves and to others, we stagnate the progress of the entire body. In this case, where we fall short, someone has to pick up our slack. This is unfair to others. Therefore, we must become accountable and responsible for our actions!

This time around, we must do things differently. If we want to become successful and sustain our prosperity, we must value our relationships. We must not ruin them because of our lack of dependability. Our goal should be to build a strong support system here on earth. We can accomplish our mission by becoming trustworthy and dependable. Then if we fall on misfortune and our finances and resources become limited, our good reputations can help sustain us! People are willing to help those who they can trust to be dependable. Are your words baseless and void, or can you be counted on to perform your obligations? Your answer determines your success or your failure in life.

Being a trustworthy, dependable person is a virtue. People love to be surrounded by those who they can trust and count on. To be trustworthy is to be reliable. Your "yes" means "yes" and your "no" means "no." Therefore, when you make commitments, you first count the cost, you accurately assess your ability to perform your obligations, and you take your commitments seriously. Dependable people think ahead about the consequences if they are unable to perform.

Before you commit yourself to anything, or anyone, you should first take healthy precautions. You should not put your well-being, or the well-being of others, at risk. Before making commitments, consider the interest of others, as well as yourself. Do not jeopardize your integrity by committing to obligations you know you cannot live up to.

Trustworthy people are mature and responsible. They don't just live for today; they also keep tomorrow in mind. Instead, they allot themselves extra time in case of a delay, and they never over-commit to anything or anyone. These people keep their priorities in order, and they recognize that reputation means more than short-term instant gratification. As a result, they protect their integrity and guard their reputation with their life. If they notice that they have a conflict, which will cause them to be unable to perform their obligations, they quickly notify the party they commit to and try to make other provisions. When problems arise, they don't run away, hide or neglect their responsibilities. Instead, they perform and live up to them; even under pressure!

It is essential that we all become trustworthy and dependable. As we change, life around us changes, too! If we live life without integrity, we will always be surrounded by drama and chaos caused by our actions. According to the Universal Law of Cause and Effect, our adverse actions will always have a negative impact on our lives. We essentially reap what we have sown. In order to sustain a good life full of peace, prosperity and joy, we must sow seeds of good behavior. A key part to building character is learning how to be dependable and trustworthy. There are many people in the world who are counting on us to perform our obligations. Therefore, it's finally time to grow up and become mature! We can accomplish this task by counting the cost of our obligations before we commit to them and performing our task in a timely fashion.

Many of us are great starters, but terrible at finishing the things we begin. We commit to jobs, schools, family members and friends. However, we end up not living up to our promises. At first our commitments are new and fun, so we tackle them with pride. Yet, as time goes on, we get bored and tired. Consequently, we give up and quit, leaving our obligations to someone else to pick up the slack.

For some of us quitting has become a normal activity. We feel no conviction or remorse for failing to perform the duties we committed to do. Instead of staying positive and doing productive things, we have quit and freed up our time to get involved with mischief. This attitude has derived from wrong thinking and lack of integrity. If we want to become successful, we can no longer live a quitter's lifestyle! Success comes with hard work and diligence. There are no shortcuts to reach the top and sustain a good living!

Anything we obtain as the result of a shortcut will ultimately be taken away from us. Therefore, shortcuts are a waste of time! They only lead back to the starting point, the beginning. We can no longer afford to make the same mistakes. Therefore, we must pull up our sleeves and begin our course steady, firm and committed. Following this principle, we only obligate ourselves to do the things we know in our hearts we can finish. We no longer use our words loosely. Today, we think about our words before we say them, and we complete the task that we start!

Dependable people are assets to anyone to whom they commit themselves. Companies thrive because of loyal, dependable employees. In organizations, dependable people can be counted on to be present daily, on time, and ready to perform their tasks. Dependable people are steady in their performance. Their work is consistent and they always perform at their best! They don't do an excellent job on Monday and drop the ball on Wednesday. Their work is their priority, so they consistently take it seriously! They know they are counted on by others, so they take pride in performing their tasks. Dependable people are the solid, deep-rooted foundation of any successful thing! Without their commitment, success would not be possible.

It is essential that when we get out of prison and obtain, then maintain, employment, we become trustworthy and dependable to the organizations to which we commit. Being an ex-felon already comes with a negative stigma. The world believes that we are highly unlikely to succeed. Let's prove them wrong!

When you get a job, look at it as a gift from God. He is giving you another chance at life. Even if it is not the job that you want right now, honor it and be dependable. As you work hard and perform your duties integrally, your light will shine! Eventually your efforts will be rewarded by God and you will be promoted. Remember, when we do good work and give our service to others, we don't just do it for people; we give our service to God! As we honor Him, He in turn honors us. If we don't get the promotion we desire from man, God will eventually open another door. Even when people aren't faithful, God is faithful! He sees and knows everything! Therefore, he is sure to reward our good efforts.

When we are expected to be at our jobs at a certain time, it is important that we arrive on time! Job schedules are created to maintain order and address the needs of the organization. When we come to work late, we are cheating our employers of time we committed to give, which may cause others distress. This is not good! Always count the cost and make provisions for possible delays. Get to work early, so you can be calm and settled when your workday begins.

If we start our mornings with chaos and confusion, it will indeed set the tone for our entire day! In order to start the day right, prepare yourself to get up early. Spend adequate time doing your daily mediations, and prepare your mind and soul for a successful day. Be alert for possible mishaps, and plan ahead to avoid them. As you do, you will be able to avoid unwarranted stress and dilemmas.

Before you open your eyes in the morning, recall to your memory all your commitments and obligations for the day. Think about what you have to do to fulfill them. Then, take necessary precautions to tackle your goals. Make it a priority to be where you have committed yourself to be, at the time you have agreed. As you become trustworthy and dependable, you will radiate with an inner sense of pride and satisfaction. Your self-confidence will increase, because within you know you are doing the right thing! In addition, those around you will also honor your efforts, and you will become a shining star!

As humans, we are not expected to be perfect. There will be times when we will be unable to execute our commitments. There may be days where uncontrollable circumstances will prevent us from going to work. As responsible individuals, we are to call ahead, as early as possible, to inform our employers about our dilemmas. In addition, we are to take others into consideration by giving them an adequate amount of time, due to our hardships, to make necessary adjustments.

There will also be times when God opens new doors of provision and we are offered better job opportunities. In that case, we are not to disappear or abandon the people and the places that helped us gain a new start. Instead, we are to give adequate notice of our resignation, which, in most cases, is done at least two weeks in advance. It is unethical to leave an organization without adequate notice! Treat your employer just as you would want someone to treat you. Never destroy relationships, especially with jobs! You may need them in the future for employment or a good reference. Therefore, don't let your actions destroy the good deeds and hard work you are leaving behind. Instead, explain your situation, thank your employer for the opportunity you were given, and maintain the good reputation you have established!

Another major problem we have in society is people don't live within their means. They commit to financial obligations that they do not have the ability or desire to pay. Many of us have lived in houses and apartments we couldn't afford. We leased or bought cars that were out of our budget range, and we charged items on our credit cards that we were unable to pay for, all to achieve instant gratification, or to please others. Then, we began to scheme and scam, and rob Peter to pay Paul, to avoid departing with the things we obtained. This cycle is burdensome and self-destructive! We must not let this fate become our portion this time around!

Therefore, we must count the cost before we agree to financial obligations. Never sign for anything that you know you are unable to pay for!

It is essential that we learn to manage and budget our finances. We may have to sacrifice today, in order to be well off tomorrow. If we live in moderation knowing tomorrow will be better, life will become more peaceful. In addition, we will build good credit that we can count on to be useful in the future.

Many of us must work on building back the trust of our family members and friends. In the past, we made many promises that we have broken. Left alone in prison, we have had the time we need to analyze our faults and re-shift our focus. As a result, we have been able to take a time out to see how our actions not only affected ourselves, but the people around us. We owe it to those who love us to turn our lives around and do the right thing. Prison has shown us who really cares and what matters the most in life. Let's get our priorities in order and change our future! We do this by rebuilding healthy family ties.

When we make verbal commitments, we no longer take them lightly. We do what we say, at the time we promise we will do something. As a result, we become support beams to those around us, and to those who love and care for us. We don't break our promises; we perform the obligations that we commit to. Today we are assets to our friends and family. Our actions set the standards for what behavior we expect in return. As we become trustworthy and dependable, those around us take our lead and do the same. Our family lives become peaceful and more enjoyable, while at the same time. we begin to feel good about "self."

Today marks a brand new day. Our experiences no longer have to be the same. We have the option to exercise our choice to be honorable people. It's important that we understand the virtue of a good reputation and make every effort not to ruin our relationships. Nobody wants to be associated with individuals who lack character. The only way to flourish is to honor your words! When you make commitments and promises to others, perform them! Do not make others have to take up your slack! Let your "yes" be "yes" and your "no" be "no." Count the cost before you agree to the terms of any obligation. When you do, you will be at peace! You will no longer have to lie or hide from others you made commitments to. You can look everyone in the face and move about life with your head held up high!

Now that we understand the importance of being trustworthy and dependable, let's take a look at some examples that will illuminate our understanding of the material we covered in this chapter.

EXAMPLE 1 -

Monica grew up in the inner city of St. Louis, Missouri. Monica's mother was a single mom who worked hard to give her child a good life. As a result, Monica grew up carefree. Her mother sheltered her from danger and worked two jobs to provide for her daughter, and Monica never went without!

Growing up, Monica felt lonely. She was often left in the house by herself while her mother worked two jobs. As a result, she turned to her friends and peers to receive the time and attention she was missing from her mother. Consequently, Monica began hanging out late. Before long, she was persuaded by others to try drugs.

First, Monica started using marijuana, but quickly graduated to cocaine; then, she tried dope. Her addiction got the best of her and she fell victim to the streets.

Monica got pregnant and had a daughter named Tara that Monica's mother was left to raise. Tara was very fond of her mother, even though Monica was seldom ever around. In Tara's eyes, Monica was her hero. She looked up to her and wanted to be just like her.

Monica would make promises to Tara all the time, and convinced her she was going to perform them. One early morning on her fifth birthday, Tara woke up early looking for Monica to take her to the circus, as Monica had promised her months in advance. Tara got all dressed up and waited patiently by the door. Hours and hours went by and Monica never showed up. After Monica failed to appear, her mother bought Tara a cake and took her to the movies to make up for Monica's broken promise. Yet, Tara was still heartbroken. Till this day she never forgot how her mother's absence hurt her. That day changed the course of Tara's whole life!

Several years passed and Monica stayed loyal to the streets. One day she got caught shoplifting to take care of her drug habit. Her shoplifting offense landed her in jail and she was sentenced to two years in prison. During Monica's prison sentence, she tried to make amends with her daughter, who was now thirteen years old. By then, Tara felt unloved and unwanted by her mother. In turn, she treated others poorly and rebelled in school.

While in prison, Monica managed to rekindle her relationship with Tara, in prison, after Monica promised to never let her down again. The two of them talked on the phone frequently and Tara would often come to visit her mother behind bars.

One day, the jail was preparing for their annual Friends and Family Day. Because Tara promised Monica she would be there, she looked forward to seeing her daughter. Monica bought picture tickets from the prison and had snacks and drinks ready to entertain her daughter. She bragged to all the inmates in her prison dorm about her daughter's beauty and intelligence. As a result, all of Monica's friends looked forward to seeing Tara.

Friends and Family Day finally arrived. Monica was up early, making preparation for the grand event. Everyone's guests began to arrive, but there was no sign of Tara. Monica sat at the neatly arranged table, looking around for her guest to appear.

Tears began to flow down Monica's face, as Family Day was close to ending and Tara had still not arrived. She dried her eyes and when she looked up she saw her mother approach.

"Monica, Monica, I made it!" Monica's mother shouted as she walked through the prison gates.

"Mommy, where is Tara?" Monica asked.

"Sit down, baby," Monica's mother said as she sat down on the bench. "Tara has a boyfriend now, who she claims she is deeply in love with. He wanted her to go with him to the park today, so she decided at the last minute not to come,"

"But she promised me, Mom. Why would she break her promise to be with some boy?" Monica questioned.

"Baby, you have done a lot in your life, and you have hurt Tara on several occasions. Don't get me wrong, your baby loves you, but the truth is she doesn't trust you. You've broken so many promises that it's hard for her, or even me for

that matter, to trust you. I'm sorry baby, but Tara says she can't stand being hurt anymore by you. So, she wants to step back until she sees you are serious," Monica's mom replied.

"But, Mom, she promised me!" Monica said as she cried.

"Yes, baby, but what about your broken promises? Do you remember your daughter's fifth birthday? I'll never forget she got all dressed up in her beautiful yellow dress, and I put long braids in her hair and tied ribbons around them. We waited and watched all day on the couch in the living room for you and you never showed up. That little girl cried her heart out. I took her to the movies, but she was still heartbroken. After that day, Tara has never been the same. Baby, you hurt her," Monica's mom said as Monica began to break down and cry.

Monica never realized the effect her behavior had on anyone, except herself. Her daughter's actions sparked her to realize how much pain she actually caused others. This became the turning point of Monica's life.

Today, Monica is reunited with her mother and daughter. She works as a counselor in a local drug rehabilitation facility, and she is drug free. Monica and Tara maintain a good relationship; they are best friends. Monica now sees the importance of her commitments and she takes them seriously!

EXAMPLE 2 -

Julie came home from prison and found it very difficult to get a job. She searched high and low, but nobody would give her a chance. Almost being violated by her parole officer for not having a job, she finally convinced Mr. Harris at the local grocery store to hire her.

It felt good to have a job. So Julie worked hard each day as a proud cashier. She maintained a pleasant attitude and all her customers bragged about her service. As a result, Mr. Harris was happy he'd made the choice to hire Julie.

After several months of working at the store, one of the customers noticed Julie's dedication to her job. He solicited Julie to work at his hardware store and promised to give her two dollars more an hour for her compensation. Julie thought about the large increase she would receive in her check and quickly decided to jump ship.

Julie was unable to face Mr. Harris to tell him she was leaving to work at the local hardware store. Consequently, she left Mr. Harris in the middle of his biggest season of the year. With few options, he had to take on her position and do it himself.

Shortly after, Julie began working at the hardware store, where she received an increase in her pay. The money was good, but her boss was very demanding. She had to work twice as hard as she had worked at the grocery store.

One day Mr. Harris came to the hardware store to make a copy of a key. Julie noticed him and couldn't even look him in the face.

"Oh, so this is why you left, you little traitor. Didn't your mother teach you anything about consideration and loyalty? I was the one that gave you a chance when you got out of prison. Nobody else would even hire you, and you do me like this," Mr. Harris shouted loudly in the store as Julie's new boss listened.

After Mr. Harris left, Julie's boss approached her. "Listen, Julie, you never told me you were in prison. What's that all about?" her boss asked.

Julie explained her story and two weeks later new boss, for no apparent reason, decided to let her go. She was devastated! Consequently, she was out of a job and had no place to turn. This taught her a HUGE lesson about being trustworthy, loyal and dependable. It took her several months to get a new job, but this time she knows how to handle matters ethically.

We are at a crossroad in life. We can stay the same, or take this time to work on and develop our character. Many of us have made promises to God and to people in our family, as well as friends, that we have broken. We have used compelling words to convince others that we were serious about change, but deep within our hearts, we had no desire to live up to our promises. Some of us have had a chance to make amends; others have messed up so bad, there is no turning back. Consequently, we ruined our Rolodex of contacts, because we have failed to uphold our commitments. Today, we have a choice; either we can remain the same, or we can make a change and become upright individuals. The choice is solely our own decision. Our deceit doesn't fool others; we only deprive ourselves.

Are you tired or burning bridges and causing others distress? Are you finally ready to commit to working on becoming a dependable, trustworthy member of society?

If so, follow me in this short prayer, *"God, I thank You for showing me how important it is to be trustworthy and dependable. I no longer want to break the promises I make to others. I want to be ethical at all times, so I will be trusted. I ask for forgiveness for anyone I may have harmed by my broken promises. I ask that You heal each person's heart, that I have let down or disappointed. Help me to be able to make amends with all those that my actions have adversely affected. Give me the strength and the courage to recognize when I'm not being honest with myself and others. Guide me on the correct path in which You wish for me to take, and give me the inner strength and ability to become a greater "self." I thank You for the character trait of being trustworthy and dependable. I now take this trait on as my own. Amen."*

You have made another huge step in your pursuit to a greater "self." Congratulations! This new character trait will take you a long way in life. Monitor your actions and do your best to always be trustworthy and dependable!

QUESTIONS

1) Why is it important to be trustworthy and dependable?
2) What happens when people cannot trust you?
3) How do we affect others when we do not perform our obligations?
4) What commitments do we have to our employers?
5) Why is it bad to take on financial obligations that we are unable to maintain?

WRITING ASSIGNMENT

I. Name three events where you have broken your commitment to others.

II. Write out how you believe your behavior effected others, in each incident.

III. Write out what you can do to make amends with those you hurt, in each incident.

CHAPTER 8
Patience That Passed the Test!

We live in a fast-paced society where most desire instant results. People want the things they want; at the time they want it! Selfish ambitions fuel the soul, continuing the cycle of self-centeredness. Caught up in the race to make it to the finish line first, few anticipate delays. Instead of waiting for the perfect solution, we create our own self-made concoctions. Consequently, our shortcuts result in compromising behavior, leading us back to the very place where we started, the beginning. It is our inability to slow down and patiently wait that becomes the pitfall which leads to our ruin.

Life is a series of tests and trials that teach us the lessons we need to grow. Without trials and tribulations, we will not develop the skill sets needed to achieve success. Our greatest teacher is actually life itself!

When we skip steps or take shortcuts, ultimately we fail! Without developing a solid foundation needed to remain steady during adversity, we will be knocked down by life's blows. Understanding this concept, we now know there are no quick fixes. There is no such thing as microwave solutions! Ultimately, we must adequately go through each test and trial. When we pass the test, we can move on to the next level. In order to be successful, we must develop patience.

In this chapter, we will explore the character trait of patience and its importance. Patience is a key attribute we all need to sustain our joy in life. By learning to develop patience we will be protected, enabling us to avoid unnecessary hardships.

Patience is the ability to wait at ease for an expected result, without becoming anxious, frustrated or wavered. Life's process largely consists of waiting. Everything transpires in steps and stages, nothing happens overnight. Waiting is a process that we cannot avoid! Most of our lives will be spent waiting for something! Having this knowledge, we must prepare ourselves for the journey of life. We equip ourselves for victory when we learn how to be patient.

In order to develop patience, we must change our mindset. Instead of trying to reach the finish line first, we must slow down and pace ourselves. Our focus should no longer be simply to accomplish our result; it must include enjoying the journey of life. Therefore, we must slow down and relax, and not be taken off guard by delays.

When we endure hardships and struggles, we are to explore them. Instead of getting frustrated or wasting our time by trying to go around them, we go through them. As a result, we no longer let life's obstacles shake us. Instead, we patiently endure! Today, we intentionally look for the good in every situation. By finding the positive points, we are able to put our minds and souls at ease. Changing our perception and how we view our dilemmas, enables us to develop patience. It is the character trait we need to make life more enjoyable, especially during rough seasons.

In order to be victorious, we must not be taken off guard by unexpected obstacles and delays. Instead, we mentally prepare ourselves to expect delays. Many times delays have a good purpose. They often prevent us from going on the wrong path in life. In this instance, they become the barriers that block us from destruction. When we are able to understand the correct perspective about delays, we no longer become rattled or frustrated when they occur. Instead we look at delays from God's perspective. They are His way of saying, "Not now." It does not mean you will not get the result that you desire; it just means you will not get it at the time you expect it. It will come, but at the appointed time!

Throughout the *Voices of Consequences Enrichment Series*, we learned about the need to be prepared for the blessings God desires to give us. Today, we know He will not give us more than we are able to handle or bear. Delays are God's way of helping us to prepare for what is yet to come. They are the periods in life where we are temporarily stagnated, so we can go through God's preparation process, which will enable us to soar in life.

The best thing we can do for ourselves during our seasons of delay is to work on "self." Instead of murmuring and complaining, we should be looking within to figure out how we can utilize this period to become a better "self." As we change, life around us also changes. When we pass our tests and trials by growing and learning the lessons God intends for us to learn, life has no choice but to propel us into our next stage of advancement. Promotion cannot be withheld when we pass the test!

When we are able to view a delay as a test, we are able to see that it may be put in our path to get our attention. When we take heed to the delay, and make the necessary changes to move ahead, we no longer have to stay stagnated. We overcome the hurdles of delay by accurately viewing their purpose, taking heed to them, and finally making the necessary changes to move ahead!

The difficulties and pain we bear today have no comparison to the rewards we stand to receive when we pass the test. When we sacrifice and develop the patience to endure, we ultimately receive our reward! As we do things correctly the first time and not take shortcuts, we won't have to repeat the same course. Instead, we pass each test and move forward! On the other hand, when we fail our test we stay stuck in the same cycle until we pass it. That means there may be a change of people and a change of environment, but we will continue to receive the same exact test until we learn the lesson. Today we no longer have to stay stagnated, repeating the same cycles of life! We now have the ability to advance by confronting our obstacles head on and conquering them!

Now that we understand the detriment of shortcuts and repeating the same negative cycles in life, we must equip ourselves with patience, so we have the ability to stand firmly during trials. We develop patience as we learn how to enjoy ourselves during our "seasons of delay."

Many of us are scared to be alone. Consequently, we do anything it takes to keep our minds occupied so we don't have to deal with "self." We dread being by ourselves because we don't want to deal with the root of our problems. Dealing with "self" is often painful. No one wants to see their inadequacies, especially when we don't know how to fix them. As a result, we avoid looking at our reflection in the mirror, so we don't have to face our own inner pain. Today, we no longer have to live life this way! We now have the knowledge of how to improve "self."

As we are delayed, we can look at our temporary dilemmas as blessings. We could have continued on the same destructive road and our fate could have resulted in death.

Congratulations! We are still alive! The gift of life means we have the ability to change our course. In this instance, the delay isn't a mishap, it's actually a blessing! It's God's way of saying, "Daughter, I have something better for you. You are special and I have chosen you for a greater purpose. I've slowed you down, not to hurt you, but for you to open your eyes and see the greater plans I have for your life." When you look at your delay from that perspective, you are able to embrace it with joy and use it for the purpose it was intended.

Working on "self" can be an enjoyable process. As you watch yourself grow and ultimately find your purpose, you will become fulfilled. The void we've been trying to fill all of our lives can be nurtured in the midst of delay. When we are forced to stop and reroute, we find the solutions we have been searching for all along. Then, we discover the obstacle we became frightened by at the first sight, was the vehicle God sent to lead us to our ultimate destination—purpose. Knowing this, we can take this time out with joy and work on our greatest asset, which is "self."

We learned in this series, the importance of mediation and analyzing the root of our problems. Meditation is essential and can be quite enjoyable. When we have delays, we can spend our time meditating. We can also assess the needs of "self." By the time we finish that process, our waiting time is up! In that case, our delay wasn't a bad thing at all. It becomes a blessing!

Time, in life, is very precious; every moment counts! In the world, we are so busy taking care of ourselves and our families that it is hard to take out the necessary time to work on "self." We often get frustrated, waiting on lines or waiting in traffic. We want to do things as quickly as possible. So, we often murmur and complain when we experience delays. This makes our obstacles more difficult to bear.

While waiting for traffic, we can pop in an inspirational tape and feed our spirits with faith. While waiting in line, we can meditate and assess our needs. While waiting for a package to arrive, we can read a self-help book. The secret is to learn how to make the best usage of our time by working on "self." As we get caught up in self-improvement, we no longer are focused on the time we have to wait. It's like the old saying, "Time flies by when we are having fun!"

As we learn how to have fun in the midst of our road-blocks, they no longer become frustrating. Mastering patience comes when we learn how to master utilizing our time. When we figure out the things we like to do by ourselves, which are productive, delays no longer bother us. When we learn to love "self" and enjoy spending time alone," we actually welcome delays. In that case, we can take a time out and give ourselves the necessary care and attention we need to advance in life!

Many of us have given up on quality results, because we refuse to wait on them. We start many projects but rarely finish them and we settle for less, primarily because we have no patience. We become desperate for results because we are seeking false idols for fulfillment. Secretly we believe in our minds if we obtain the things we want now, we will be happy. This is a terrible misconception which keeps us caught up in the chase. When we are able to realize satisfaction and fulfillment only come from within, we will not look on the outside for results. Instead of becoming bored with "self," we realize we are our number one asset! Therefore, we enjoy the opportunity for self-improvement. Today we realize by being patient, we begin to enjoy the process of life, which makes obstacles easier to bear. In addition, we no longer look to others to give us the things we can obtain within. Coming into alignment with "self" helps us to identify our correct priorities in life. As a result, our perspective about circumstances and events becomes clearer and we develop patience that enables us to be victorious!

When we develop patience, we become tolerant of others. We give people the freedom to grow and discover life at their own pace. As a result, we are no longer bothered by the inadequacy of others around us. We love people for who they are, yet we do not let their inefficiencies affect "self." Instead, we protect ourselves by creating boundaries. Our focus is no longer trying to control and change people, making them the way we see fit. Instead, we take out the time we need to improve "self." As we become fulfilled within, we are sustained!

Today, we no longer look to get our strength or happiness from people, who will ultimately fail us. We now look to our "Higher Power" for provision. He leads and guides us into the direction we should go, and we become independent of people. We realize we can lead the horse to the well, but we cannot make it drink. Therefore, we warn others when they are in the pathway of destruction. If they don't take heed to our warnings, we lovingly detach. We don't join them on their path of destruction. Instead, we take care of ourselves, by getting out of the way. In this instance, we love without becoming destructive to our biggest asset, which is "self."

In this season, we are taking back our power to succeed! We have learned how to surrender to God and the processes of life. As a result, we don't get frustrated or discouraged when obstacles arise. Instead, we rejoice! We now realize our obstacles are opportunities to advance. Therefore, we no longer murmur and complain.

Today, we pray and look for God's divine guidance. We do not try to change people, dress them up and make them into what we want them to be. Instead, we give everyone the freedom to grow and the chance to realize the things that are important in life. In addition, we no longer scheme and scam our way through life, looking for a shortcut. We now take our time and do things the right way, so we only have to do them once. Congratulations! We are no longer bound. We do the right things, at all times, so we know positive results are on the way!

Now that we know the virtue of patience, let's explore some real life examples to bring more light to what we have learned in this chapter.

EXAMPLE 1 -

Cassandra met Michael in school and they became high school "sweethearts." She felt in her heart that she had met her soul mate. Michael was very smart and ambitious. He believed he should work hard to get the things he wanted in life. He shared his views with Cassandra and inspired her to go away to college.

The couple stayed together and Michael pushed his way through college. Cassandra got discouraged by the financial hardships she endured getting through college. She believed she should quit and get a good job, yet Michael convinced her not to. Cassandra took his advice, but was distracted from her goal when she met Brian.

Brian was a big-time drug dealer who would often drive up to her college campus in his brand new Mercedes Benz. The girls on campus became excited when Brian came around. Everyone seemed to want to be his girlfriend, but he chose Cassandra. At first, she rejected Brian because of her love for Michael. Yet, after Brian took her on a few dates and showered her with gifts, Cassandra cheated on her true love, Michael, to be with Brian.

Almost instantly, Cassandra got caught up in the "high life." She loved the luxurious lifestyle Brian afforded her, so she dropped out of school, dumped Michael, and eventually became pregnant with Brian's baby.

Life was grand for a few years. Cassandra got everything she wanted in her title as a drug dealer's main girlfriend. Four years into the relationship, Cassandra and Brian got caught up into a drug conspiracy and were charged in Federal Court for conspiracy to sell drugs, even though no actual drugs were found on them.

Cassandra lost her baby to social services and is now serving a seven-year sentence in Federal prison. During her incarceration, she was able to take a time out to reevaluate her past choices. She still stays in contact with Michael, who is now married and is a successful engineer. He sends her letters of support and money orders on occasion. Cassandra greatly regrets her decision not to stay in school and wishes she still had a chance to spend the rest of her life with Michael. She now realizes shortcuts only bring about mishaps, so she has developed the character trait of patience.

EXAMPLE 2 -

Monique grew up in Hartford, Connecticut, and fell victim to a lifestyle of heavy drug usage. She would often go on "get high sprees" that would last for weeks at a time.

Monique's only care in life became obtaining her drug of choice, "heroin." Monique received several warnings to change her lifestyle, yet she didn't take heed to any of them. She became so wrapped up in drug usage, she could no longer think straight.

The cops did a random drive by and Monique got caught in the back of a car with drugs and paraphernalia. She was arrested and sent downtown to the county jail. Afraid to kick the habit, Monique did everything she could to get out of jail. She called all of her relatives and friends, but no one agreed to bail her out. Monique tried to be content with the process she was going through, until the pain kicked in.

Monique made one last call to an old boyfriend. She made several promises and he agreed to bail her out. To her dismay, the ex-boyfriend came down to the jail and the computer system was down, so he was unsuccessful. Monique stayed persistent and got him to return when the system came back up again. But the jail didn't take cash, so he had to wait until the morning to get a money order.

Several days went by and Monique couldn't get in touch with her friend. Her instincts said it was time to take a time out, instead of returning to the streets. However, Monique refused to listen to her inner voice and continued to call her ex-boyfriend, until he finally came to get her. Monique was overjoyed to be bailed out of jail after serving two weeks. Immediately, she went back to the streets, where she got high. Monique was so happy to have her idol, heroin, back in her hands that she obtained as much of it as she could get.

Only twenty-four hours from being bailed out of the county jail, Monique overdosed on heroin and died.

Monique viewed jail as a nuisance or a delay, but actually it was the place meant to save her soul from destruction. Consequently, her incorrect thinking ultimately led to her death.

Thank God we don't have the same fate as Monique! We have all been blessed with the gift of life! Let's honor it and gain the attribute of patience, so we can be successful! Delays are sent as anchors of help from our "Higher Power." Therefore, let's grab a hold of them and use our time to help us become more productive people. This time doesn't have to be against us. Let's use our power and make it work for us!

Are you ready to use your time wisely and begin to tap into your potential? You can start today by taking patience on as a character trait!

If you are ready to change follow me in this prayer, *"God, I thank You for the insight You have given me about patience. I now realize delays are sent at times, to protect me and help me stay on the right course. It is during these intervals that I can work on becoming a greater "self." I thank You for giving me the correct perspective about delays, and I thank You for giving me the strength of patience to endure. Lead and guide me unto the correct path of life. Shut doors that will lead to my danger or destruction and open doors that will lead to my success. Give me divine wisdom and knowledge to know what to do, and how to do it, at your correct appointed time. I thank You now for my new character trait of patience. Today I embrace it and it will sustain me all the days of my life! Amen."*

Congratulations! You have made another great victory in your pursuit to a greater "self." Your new character trait of patience will take you places you never imagined you would climb. Guard this information with your heart. You are now equipped to soar!

QUESTIONS
1) What is patience?
2) Why is patience important?
3) What is God's purpose for delays?
4) How can we benefit from delays?
5) How do we stay calm during periods of delays?
6) How do we become patient and tolerant with people?

WRITING ASSIGNMENT

    I. Write out three events that your lack of patience got the best of you.

    II. List what you missed out on by not having patience, for each event.

_____

    III. List what you would now do differently, for each event.

_____

CHAPTER 9-
Kindness that Overcomes Evil

I t is human nature to seek revenge on those who try to abuse us, or who threaten to step in the way of our advancement. The old saying, "An eye for an eye," is the normal code of society. Consequently, we may get caught up in a vicious cycle of inflicting pain on one another. Instead of being filled with love, the world becomes filled with hate. Most are only interested in the things from which they stand to benefit. This self-centered mentality prevents us from having mercy on our neighbors and uplifting them. Instead of being kind, gentle, and loving, we become angry, harsh and bitter to others. As we sow these seeds of negativity into the universe, they eventually return back to hit us when we least expect it. This is not the way God purposed us to live! We were all created to be loving, caring individuals. We honor God with our service when we are kind to one another.

In this chapter, we will learn the virtue of being kind. The character trait of kindness is very powerful! It has the ability to pierce the hearts of even our enemies. Instead of fighting fire with fire, we will learn how to utilize kindness as a weapon to overcome evil. As you absorb the information in this chapter and apply it to your life, you will position yourself to soar!

Kindness is an act of care and concern for another. It consists of taking into account the interest of our neighbors and offering our support, when needed. To be kind is to be merciful and forgiving to others. Regardless of what people do, we know that we have reached a level of maturity when we are still able to be kind to them.

When we are kind to our neighbors, we show them respect and appreciation. As we honor God, we also honor those who have authority over us by respecting them. In addition, we respect those who we come in daily contact with. We purposely watch our tone of voice and greet one another with a pleasant attitude. Instead of ripping or pulling our neighbors down, we lift them up! We find ways to encourage and compliment others in their achievements, while keeping our hearts and our motives pure. As a result, our acts of kindness are done out of the pureness of our hearts, with no expectation of something in return.

We are to be kind to others, simply because we know it is the right thing to do. Therefore, our acts of kindness are not bogus. We treat everyone with respect and generosity. As a result, the recipients of our kindness recognize our sincerity, which sparks joy within them.

When we are kind to others, we ignite the cycle of love, becoming vessels whom God is able to shine His light through. As a result, we captivate the hearts of others. When we operate in the cycle of love, we are propelled into purpose. Our acts of kindness lead us unto the road of fulfillment, causing God to reward us with satisfaction from within.

Throughout the *Voices of Consequences Enrichment Series*, we have emphasized the importance of changing our perspective in life from being self-centered to being God-centered. We learned that when we change our ways, and work according to God's principles, we open the doorway of provision. As we become kind to our neighbors, we charge the atmosphere with positive energy. As a result, our acts of love become powerful, and we open the gateway of love to be abundantly showered back down on us! It is the power of love that will sustain us, even when everything else around us fails. We fuel our love with acts of kindness. As we are kind to others our love intensifies. We begin to feel good about ourselves, because we are walking in our purpose.

Being kind is being considerate of others, yet at the same time taking care of "self." We are not to neglect our own needs to please or satisfy someone else. We help others, whenever we are able to, without neglecting ourselves. In addition, we no longer impose our agendas on others. We give everyone the freedom to be who they are, and to grow at their own pace, while at the same time, we maintain our standards of integrity.

Being kind does not mean being ignorant or allowing ourselves to be used. We must never become caretakers of healthy people who have the ability to work hard and care for themselves. Therefore, we no longer disable people by doing things for them that they should do for themselves. Instead, we are kind to others by inspiring and encouraging them to grow. As an act of kindness, we show people how to do things that help them improve "self." In this season, like the old saying, "We teach others how to fish; we do not fish for them!"

We learned in this series that obstacles are often sent to help us recognize our faults and to propel us to grow. We also learned that God is the One who authorizes obstacles and uses them to strengthen us. Therefore, we allow people to learn from their own mistakes. When they encounter obstacles, it is for a reason! Therefore, we no longer rescue people from dilemmas that are intended to help them grow. If we do, we are essentially putting our hands in the way of God's work. When we interfere with God's plans, we are automatically in violation, which puts us in danger. Consequently, we risk being punished along with the person we attempt to help.

Take a moment to think. Has there been a time in your life when everything seemed to be going fine? Then, someone whom you cared about had a problem and you offered to assist them. That person may have been experiencing a dilemma that you could easily solve, so you decided to become their rescuer. Yet, after you helped this person, it seemed like everything around you started going wrong.

When we get in God's way by helping someone whom He intends on teaching a lesson, we put ourselves at risk! In this instance by helping them, we are saying to God, "I am willing to also suffer in their consequences or punishment." Many of us are in the situations we are in today because we stepped into someone's fire.

Being kind to others means to be led by God on what we should, or should not, do for a person. Before we agree to get involved in helping someone out, we should always consult our "Higher Power." Then, He will guide us in the proper way to assist them. Today, we know we should never promote the adverse behavior of others. Therefore, we do not assist someone who is doing something that is not good. If we do, our help joins us to their adverse behavior. Consequently, we open the doors to be punished for our participation, because our help makes us an accomplice. Just like the legal system, accomplices can also be charged for a crime.

In this season, we must learn how to care and protect "self." We must not allow ourselves to be harmed by participating in adverse behavior. Instead, we must use this time to work on "self" and set boundaries. Never again are we to put our well-being at risk, because we want to please or help a friend. Today, we set healthy boundaries, and we refuse to participate in activities that can potentially cause us harm. That is the true meaning of caring for "self!"

Being kind to others is our act of service to God. It does not mean we must become attached to people. We are to perform our acts as a gift of service; then we are able to depart. Kindness doesn't mean we have to stay bound to a person and their problems. We can give them a kind word of encouragement; a gift of value they may need. Then, we are free to depart. Kindness is helping people to help themselves. It is not doing work for people that they should do for themselves. Today, we know we are not obligated to put the weight of the world on our shoulders. Life lessons have taught us it is dangerous to try to play God's role in people's lives. As a result, we are led by God in our acts of kindness. We know we are doing things correctly when we become fulfilled inside. God gives us an inner sense of peace and joy when He is happy with our service. As we feel this peace, we know our actions are pleasing to God.

It is vital that when people misuse us, harm us or treat us wrong, we are able to forgive them. Forgiveness is an act of kindness. Just because someone has done us wrong doesn't mean we must inflict pain back on them in return. When someone mistreats us, it is our cue to detach. Detachment in this case doesn't have to be permanent, unless it is necessary. We detach to protect ourselves from further harm and to allow that person time to correct their poor behavior. In this case, when we detach, we are to pray that God touches the heart of our attackers and help them to see what they've done wrong. We should also pray that God helps us to forgive the person and lead us how to resolve the matter. We are never to allow our emotions to get the best of us! When we do, we only fuel the fire and join in the negative cycle. By responding adversely, we actually attach ourselves and open the doors for punishment. God promises to take vengeance on those who do us wrong. We are not to try and perform His role; that can be dangerous! Instead, we turn our problems over to God, and let Him do His work! God's punishment to our enemies is fiercer than anything we could do ourselves. He created them; so He knows just how to change their hearts! After we take the person that has harmed us into prayer, we must forgive them.

Forgiveness keeps our hearts clean, so we can receive the blessings God has for us. When we refuse to forgive others, God in turn refuses to forgive us. Without forgiveness our lives become open to condemnation and misery. Therefore, we have no choice but to forgive!

Forgiveness is the way we detach from the negativity of others. When we forgive a person we break the chains that hold us emotionally bound to our enemies. As a result, we no longer replay their negative acts continuously in our minds. Instead, we recognize how harmful getting stuck in negativity can be for our own lives, so we intentionally let it go! This enables us to remove ourselves from our attackers permanently and put our focus back on to working on our "self."

Forgiving is not forgetting a person's actions. When we forgive, we surrender that person to God and remove all malice out of our hearts. We do not return to our attackers, especially if they have not changed their ways. If we do, we can potentially put ourselves at risk. When we forgive, we do not hold grudges. Yet, at the same time, we protect "self."

True forgiveness means we have the ability to be kind to our attackers. When we are kind to them, we are not condoning or supporting their behavior. Yet, we are able to express how we feel about what they have done, and kindly recommend they change their ways. Our dialogue is an act of kindness that is done with love, but, at the same time, we guard "self" from any further wounds. When properly done, our kind acts to our enemies pierce their hearts and cause them to recognize their bad behavior. It's important to remember we cannot change people, only God can! By praying and allowing people the freedom of expression to be who they are, that's when change actually occurs. Instead of using our efforts in vain, inflicting pain back on others, with hopes that they will change, we are to surrender that person to God in prayer. When we surrender our enemies over to God that becomes an act of forgiveness. When we learn how to properly forgive others, we learn how to become better people. Not only do we help ourselves, we also help those who harmed us. Our prayers radiate into heaven. In return, God uses obstacles and circumstances to change the hearts of our enemies. Therefore, there is power in forgiveness! It creates REAL change!

Never forget when people inflict pain upon us, it is generally not of their own doing. These people are plagued with wrong thinking and are pawns of the enemy of our soul. The enemy's mission is to steal, kill and destroy. He cannot work without the assistance of humans on this earth. Therefore, he uses people by planting negative thoughts in their minds, which the person takes on as their own. That is why some hate others without having a real reason. This occurs because their minds have become the workshop of the enemy. His thoughts are played over continuously in their minds and they take them on as their own. These people inflict pain onto others out of ignorance; they have been deceived by the enemy!

Many of us has been beat down and battered in life. Therefore, we know how it feels to be used, abused and done unjustly. We also know how it feels to be counted out. Therefore, we must break this destructive cycle by allowing the compassion and care that God has shown to us, to be shared with others who are experiencing hardships. As we are kind to others in their time of need, our action honors God. Then, He is able to use us to shine His marvelous light on those who are suffering, sparking a change within their hearts. It is our acts of kindness that have the power to tear down the walls of a demented heart. When a heart is open, it is then able to be healed by the power of love. As a result, kindness prepares one's heart to receive the ultimate healing power of God!

Now that we understand the importance of being kind to others, and we understand the correct ways to express our kindness, let's explore some examples that illustrate the power of kindness.

EXAMPLE 1-

Latoya had a little sister named Gina, whom she practically raised. Latoya was always loving and kind to Gina. She did everything she could to help her sister advance in life. Unfortunately, Gina strayed away from the guidance of her parents and got caught up in a lifestyle of drugs and gang violence. Gina's boyfriend was the leader of a gang. He got her involved in the organization, and the two enforced orders throughout their hometown of Miami, Florida.

Latoya was aware of her sister's adverse behavior, but she refused to condone it. Gina had a baby girl with her boyfriend and often sought others to care for this child, while she engaged in her gang activity. Latoya refused to help, causing Gina to become very bitter and angry towards her. She felt Latoya had abandoned her and didn't love her anymore. But, in actuality, it hurt Latoya deeply to see Gina live such a dangerous lifestyle. Her biggest fear was to hear her sister was killed in a gang war. Latoya was a woman of great faith. She would often go to church and pray for her sister to change her life.

One day, while sitting on her front porch, Gina was shot by a random shooter. She made it to the hospital where she was placed in Intensive Care. Gina felt her family hated her, so she didn't supply them as an emergency contact. Yet, one of Latoya's friends, who worked in the hospital, spotted Gina. She immediately called Latoya and informed her of the news.

Latoya and her parents rushed to the hospital. They were bedside when Gina woke up from her surgery. Gina's family stayed with her the whole time she was hospitalized, and cared for her daughter.

Latoya would come to the hospital every morning and comb Gina's hair, just like she did when she was a little girl. She would also read her healing scriptures from the Bible and talk about the importance of establishing a relationship with God. Latoya's kind words, care and compassion caused tears to roll out of Gina's eyes. Hooked up to several machines, and suffering from intense injuries, she recognized how badly her adverse choices effected her life. Even so, Latoya didn't badger Gina about the mistakes she'd made. Instead, Latoya expressed her love and told Gina how much she meant to her. As a result, Gina decided to denounce her gang affiliation.

Gina's daughter's father was furious when Gina got out of the gang. They didn't speak for several months, until he got locked up on an attempted murder charge. While imprisoned, he reached out to Gina who was then a faithful Christian. She ministered the Gospel to him and led her daughter's father to change his life. Just as Latoya had prayed for Gina, she prayed for her daughter's father. The results were amazing!

Today, Gina's daughter's father is the head of a non-profit organization that helps to deter youth from gang violence. His change has sparked many others to follow his path. The cycle of love initiated by Latoya has changed many lives!

EXAMPLE 2-

Ruth was in an abusive relationship with a man named Thomas, whom she was deeply in love with. Yet, she found it hard to separate from him. Consequently, Thomas would often beat her. When she got up enough courage to leave, he would cry, apologize and beg her not to go.

This cycle continued until one day Thomas beat Ruth so badly that she ended up with a black eye and two broken ribs. As a result, she was taken to a hospital and referred to a Woman's Shelter. Faced with the severity of her problem, she finally decided to separate from Thomas. Ruth left behind everything she worked hard for and started her life over again. As she realized how many years she'd lost being with Thomas, she grew bitter and began to hate him. Filled with bitterness and malice, Ruth was often depressed. She experienced numerous problems and found it hard to get back on her feet. One day, Ruth's counselor at the Women's Shelter invited her to attend a workshop about the power of forgiveness. That day Ruth came to realize if she didn't forgive Thomas, she would be chained emotionally to him for life. Armed with this vital information, Ruth decided to finally forgive Thomas and move ahead with her life.

As Ruth forgave Thomas, she experienced peace. As a result, things began to work out well in her life, and she got back on her feet. Ruth met a nice man at her college and the two decided to date.

One night on her way home from class, driving home with a friend, she saw Thomas's car on the side of the road. His hazard lights were blinking, while he stood outside of the car in the pouring rain, thumbing for help. At first, Ruth drove by, yet she suddenly had a change of heart. So, she drove back around and stopped for Thomas, who she hadn't seen in over two years.

He had run out of gas, so Ruth took him to the gas station to get gas for his car.

Thomas was shocked to see Ruth, whom he had searched for many years. He was even more astonished to see how kind she was to him, despite his past actions. After Thomas got the gas, he asked for Ruth's number and contact information. Ruth opted not to exchange any information, but she gave Thomas kind words of encouragement and wished him well in life.

A year passed, and Ruth got married to the man she met at school. Ruth and her husband went to their friend's church and Ruth was amazed to see Thomas, who was a deacon in the church. After the service, he walked up to Ruth and told her how after she helped him on the side of the road his heart was convicted. He apologized to her for all the harm he caused her, and shared how he dedicated his life to God and gave up his old ways.

Ruth gladly accepted his apology. That day, she realized the strength of the power of her forgiveness!

Kindness is the act we use to overcome evil. It keeps our hearts clean and pure. We overcome when we learn to be kind to others, especially those who have done us wrong. Being kind is not always easy. No one wants to be treated unfairly. When we realize the power that we have over evil, we must make the choice to be kind. It is our weapon to victory!

Are you tired of losing battles over your enemies? Are you ready to receive the definite answer that will put you on top, no matter what adverse situations you encounter? If so, follow me in this short prayer: *"God, I thank You for showing me the importance of kindness. Help me to always have a clean heart with pure motives. Direct me in ways I can daily be kind to others. Allow my kindness to be effective and let it pierce the hearts of those who receive it. Give me the strength to be kind to even those who wrongfully mistreat me. Soften my heart and teach me how to always forgive others, and show me how to be genuine in my efforts. I thank You now for your guidance, and I welcome kindness in my heart as a permanent character trait. May my kindness be effective and utilized as a weapon against evil. Amen."*

Congratulations! You have made another huge step in your pursuit to a greater "self." You now have the power of kindness to pierce hearts wherever you go. Don't take this character trait lightly. Utilize it as much as you can as your service to God!

QUESTIONS

1) What is kindness?
2) Why is kindness important?
3) Are we being kind to others when we allow them to use and abuse us? Why, or why not?
4) How do we know what we should or should not do for a person?
5) What is forgiveness?
6) How do we forgive those who mistreated us?

WRITING ASSIGNMENT

I. Write out three acts, committed by three separate people, where you've been mistreated by others.

II. Write whether or not you've forgiven this person,and list why or why not?

III. After reading this chapter, write down a way you can be kind to each person you listed that mistreated you, without causing harm to yourself.

CHAPTER 10
Self-Control That Creates Rulers

We live in a society where it is common for people to act and react based on their emotions. When people threaten our advancement or our peace, we naturally react to protect our self-interest. Sometimes our reactions can be dangerous or volatile. In this instance, we get so caught up in our feelings that one situation can cause our total ruin! After the smoke clears and we have a moment to reflect, we are able to realize how badly we reacted. Then, we become remorseful for our actions, wishing we could go back in time and take back what we did. Since reversing the clock is impossible, we are left to deal with shame, guilt and regret, all because we failed to think before we reacted!

Throughout the Voice of Consequences *Enrichment Series*, we have dealt with the importance of the mind, and controlling our emotions. We discovered the root of many of our problems comes from "stinking thinking," and the inability to master controlling "self." We have worked intensely on self-discovery and have gained in-depth knowledge on how to fix our character flaws.

In this chapter, we will learn the importance of our emotions and practicing self-control. We can work vigorously and obtain our goals, but one bad reaction can jeopardize everything that we have worked so hard to gain! In order to sustain our success, it is vital that we learn how to master our emotions and control ourselves, regardless of the circumstances we encounter. When we learn how to control "self," we become truly empowered!

Our mind is the ruler of our body. Before we do anything, it must first become a thought. After we think, we act based on our thoughts. Therefore, if our minds are flooded with wrong thoughts, which is essentially "stinking thinking," our actions will be adverse. The only way to change our actions is to change our thinking! It is the goal of this series to shed light on the incorrect thought patterns that we have established in the past. As we identify and dethrone them, we are ultimately empowered!

In the last chapter, we discussed how people who have betrayed, or harmed, us have been used by the enemy of our souls. We learned how the enemy floods the human mind with bad thoughts that we may often take on as our own. Consequently, we may act on those negative thoughts and do harmful things to others. Until we are brought into enlightenment, we may be subjected to the works of the enemy. We no longer have to stay a victim to "stinking thinking!" When negative thoughts come in our minds, we must not react. Instead, we are to discard them. We remove bad thoughts by purposely looking for the good in every situation and by dwelling on positive thoughts.

When problems arise that cause us to become angry or frightened, we must immediately try and remove ourselves from the situation and attempt to control our thoughts. Instead of trying to deal with our problems ourselves, we now have the help of our "Higher Power." As we take our problems to Him in prayer, He reveals to us divine solutions to handle our dilemmas.

When we are able to properly assess our situation in meditation, we avoid the consequences of reacting incorrectly, by taking matters in our own hands. With a clear mind, we have the ability to conquer any obstacle we may encounter. We become mature individuals when we are no longer controlled by our emotions. It is now our goal to be led by the wisdom of God!

Mastering our emotions is a skill that is developed over time. As we tap into the power of "self," and discover the areas we need to work on and address them, we are able to protect ourselves from hidden pitfalls. The enemy of our souls is very clever. He lays and watches our development. He knows our shortcomings and our weaknesses, so he plays on them. If he knows we are quick to get angry, and we easily react to those who irritate us, the enemy of our souls will attack us, using those very weaknesses. Consequently, when we are unable to control our emotions, we immediately fall for the bait, and react as the enemy intends us to. As a result, we have to pay the consequences for our adverse behavior. Now that the enemy's plans have been exposed, we no longer have to take the bait!

For all negative behavior, there are equal consequences. We learned that we reap what we sow. Therefore, even if someone did something bad to us that causes us to react adversely, we still have to pay the cost. When we inflict pain on others, we sow the same seed to return to us. In the last chapter, we learned when people do bad things to us, we are to pray for them and forgive them. Under no circumstance are we to take revenge on others. Instead, we are to care for "self" and seek God to provide a solution. When we join others in adverse behavior, we open ourselves up to punishment, which is a consequence. Therefore, we break the cycle of negativity by detaching and seeking our "Higher Power." When we learn to make detaching and seeking God a habit, we learn the skill set of self-control.

As we increase our time in prayer and meditation, we are able to train our minds to be focused on positive thoughts. This empowers us! When we have a positive state of mind, the things that used to bother us, no longer have the power to disturb us. Therefore, we no longer fall into traps that the enemy has set. It's like the mouse who sees the mouse trap and knows it is a set up. Instead of being greedy and trying to get the small piece of cheese that is on the trap, the mouse becomes wise and realizes the cheese will cost him his life. As a result, he walks away and avoids his ruin. Today, we are wise, just like the mouse who avoids the trap. Our enlightenment has brought about a new way of thinking. We now see the hidden traps, blocks ahead, so we can avoid them! We no longer do things that are contrary to the way God intends for us to live. As a result, the godly principles we live by protect us from evil and harm.

The more time we spend working on "self," which includes developing a relationship with our "Higher Power," our purpose is revealed. As a result, we no longer become distracted by people, places and things, because we are able to set our priorities in order and maintain our balance.

Mastering our emotions requires spending time daily in meditation. To strive in life, we must constantly rid ourselves of negative thoughts. Just as it is essential to take a bath on a daily basis to remain clean, we must cleanse our minds daily by meditating. If not, we will not become over-powered by negative thinking.

One of the major problems that many of us must deal with is handling our anger. Life has dealt us many blows, so we've learned to survive and protect ourselves by using our physical strength. To many of us, fighting to defend ourselves has become a way of life. We do not have to live this way anymore! We now know we have God as our Partner. He will defend us better than we ever could! When we take matters into our own hands, we block God from moving on our behalf. When we react to adversity negatively, our actions say to God, "I don't need You. I can handle this." Consequently, we block our greatest means of help.

When we encounter problems with others, we are not to let people change our good nature. If we let people take us out of character, we give them control over us. We take back our power when we learn how to properly respond to others. We don't have to always agree with what people say or do, but there is a way to express our discontentment. When people get angry and shout, or yell, we don't have to respond the same way back. We can stop them and politely say, "Listen, I don't want to argue with you. I would like to talk to you and express my feelings, but I don't want to do it in a hostile manner. I'm not looking to create problems with you."

When you talk to people in a civilized manner and kindly express your concerns, they become more willing to listen. It is very hard to fight with someone who refuses to get angry. If that person continues yelling or speaking in a loud manner, you can say, "Listen, I'm going to stop this now before things gets out of hand. When you calm down, we can discuss this later." Then, walk away.

Always remember the old saying, "It takes two to Tango!" In order to fight there must be two willing opponents. When you refuse to engage in an argument by speaking in a kind manner, your actions put out the fire!

Today, we are empowered to overcome adversity! Instead of using our fists as weapons, we now use our mind and our voice of reason. We diffuse negativity with our kindness, and we speak to our opponents and explain our concerns politely.

As a result, our voice of reason becomes the energy that diffuses negativity and puts out the flame of adversity. Our kind acts open the eyes of our opponents and eventually turn them into friends. Today we are wise and empowered because we know just how to deal with every form of adversity. When problems arise that we are unable to handle, we step back and allow the true Problem Solver to step up! We now know we can overcome any situation by the power of prayer!

Now that we understand the importance of self-control and have learned techniques to diffuse our anger, let's take a look at some up and close examples that will illuminate what we've learned in this chapter.

EXAMPLE 1-

Veronica and Lori are housed together in the same dorm at Dublin Federal Correctional Institution in California. Veronica is an outgoing, bright, friendly person. She has done her best to make the most out of her time in prison. She is very supportive to the other girls in the prison. As a result, she is greatly liked.

Lori was bitter and angry about her imprisonment. Lori's own sister set her up with a Federal agent who Lori sold three kilos of cocaine to. As a result, Lori was sentenced to an eighty-six-month prison term. Her sister's betrayal caused Lori not to trust anyone. Inside, she was very bitter and looked for opportunities to express her anger.

One day Lori and Veronica were both in the bathroom together. Veronica smiled at Lori as she washed her hands. Lori became very upset and said some nasty words to her. Veronica snapped back and the two girls were ready to fight. In the midst of the confusion, Veronica caught herself, and spoke to Lori kindly.

"Listen, Lori, why are we fighting? I smiled at you only to say good morning. Why would you get so mad and curse me out like you did?"

Lori thought about Veronica's words and she spoke back. "Well, I thought you were trying to be funny. I always see you smiling at me. What do you think, I'm stupid? I saw you talking about me to Keisha," Lori said in an angry tone.

"No, Lori, I wasn't talking bad about you. I told Keisha you have beautiful eyes. You really remind me of my cousin back home who I am very close with. That's why every time I see you I smile," Veronica stated politely.

"Oh, my goodness Veronica, I'm so sorry. I thought you were trying to insult me," Lori apologized.

"No, I just think you are very pretty," Veronica replied.

"Wow. Thank you. I'm sorry for reacting as I did," Lori stated.

"Me too! I'm very sorry," Veronica replied as the two girls gave each other a hug.

Today Lori and Veronica are best friends. Lori has been able to learn a lot from Veronica. She's now accepted her prison term as an opportunity to advance, and she is no longer angry and bitter. Lori has gotten her GED and just got accepted to the Residential Drug Treatment Program, which will take twelve months off her sentence.

Veronica is on her way home. She has two months left in prison. She now realizes the importance of properly reacting to people. Her interaction with Lori enlightened her how to use her voice of reason to stop unnecessary arguments.

EXAMPLE 2-

Renee recently got out of prison and landed a job as a receptionist at a doctor's office, where she is making good money. *Her boss, Dr. Traedger, is a very busy pediatrician who has a lot of clients.*

Every day, Renee encounters screaming children and busy phones. At times, it can get very hectic, and Renee often goes home exhausted. Challenged by the job, Renee contemplated quitting, but she decided to hold on.

One day, Dr. Traedger came to work and insulted Renee. He told her she was useless and didn't deserve the pay that she got. Renee's face turned beet red. Inside, she was absolutely furious! She wanted to jump and choke Dr. Traedger, curse him out and quit her job. It took everything in her to refrain from reacting adversely.

Instead of screaming, Renee decided to smile and keep her mouth shut. She finished up the day and went home, where she shut the door of her room, fell on her knees, and prayed to her "Higher Power."

The next day, Renee went to work as usual and performed to the best of her ability. Dr. Traedger's office assistant was out on sick leave, so Renee took over the tasks of the office. She organized all the patient's charts and made sure everything ran smoothly.

At the end of the day, Dr. Traedger came up to Renee and apologized to her for what happened the day before. He admitted that he was having personal problems at home, and he wrongly took his anger out on her. Then, he complimented her on her work ethic and her ability to stay calm when he scolded her. Renee accepted his apology and felt relieved.

Five years have gone by and Renee still works for the doctor. She is no longer a receptionist. Today, she is Dr. Traedger's medical assistant. She makes very good money and her boss is paying for her school tuition, so she can get her LPN license. Not only is Dr. Traedger her boss, he is also Renee's friend and biggest supporter.

Renee is so glad she didn't respond adversely to Dr. Traedger when he was rude to her unjustly. She sees how taking control over her emotions and taking her problems to God in prayer has had positive results.

Renee and Veronica are no different than you and I. These young ladies stood up and decided to take control over their emotions. As a result, they both were blessed and rewarded.

Today, we have the opportunity to choose who will control our lives. Will we let people control us with their adverse actions? Or, will we take control over our minds and how we respond to others?

If you are ready to take self-control on as a character trait to sustain success in life, follow me in this prayer: *"God, I thank You for showing me the importance of self-control. I ask You to help me control my thoughts. Rid me of all negative thinking. Fill my mind with thoughts from You. Help me to stay focused on doing the right thing at all times, regardless of what people say or do to me. Give me Your divine direction when I stand in the midst of adversity. Help me to become a vessel that is filled with Your love, so that my acts of kindness can pierce the hearts of others. Help me to always be a voice of reason that can tear down the strongholds of "stinking thinking." When I speak, give me the words to say that will allow others to clearly see my point of view. Help me to know when I am right and when I'm wrong. When I go off course, gently nudge me and guide me back on the right track. I thank You now for the character trait of self-control. I now receive it into my life. Amen."*

Congratulations! You made another huge step in your pursuit to a greater "self." Self-control will now help you to stay calm, even in the midst of adversity. When others react adversely, you will know how to remain calm. As a result, you will have the ability to always be a victor, instead of becoming a victim! You now have self-control that will make you a ruler in life!

DISCUSSION QUESTIONS
1) What is self-control?
2) Why is self-control so important?
3) How do we manage our emotions?
4) Why are our thoughts so powerful?
5) How do we diffuse our anger?
6) What should we do if we face problems with people?

WRITING ASSIGNMENT
I. Describe three events where you let your emotions get the best of you. What was the result of your behavior?

II. Describe three events where you wanted to explode, but you kept your composure. How did you benefit from your behavior?

CHAPTER 11
The Importance of Peace

We live in a fast-paced world that is very competitive. People are focused on reaching their desired destination, believing this goal will bring them fulfillment. In the race to the finish line, we often run into road blocks. These obstacles are sent by God to get His children back on the right track. Not understanding God's great plan for our lives, our instinct is to fight against His will. As a result, we come up with crafty plans to divert obstacles. Consequently, we may successfully remove the very barriers that were put in place to save us from destruction. Blinded by worldly ambitions, we are often unable to see the danger in our behavioral patterns. Refusing to take heed to all the warnings, we manipulate our way out of dilemmas only to encounter another one, which becomes even more intense. This cycle continues to repeat. As a result, there is never a peaceful moment.

Peace doesn't come until we learn how to surrender. As long as we continue to believe our way is correct, we close the door to change. Peace only arrives when we surrender our own self-ambitious plans for the will of God. Until we make that choice, constant obstacles will continue to arise. Remember, obstacles are God's way of saying, "Daughter, you are on the wrong path!" As we open our eyes and take heed to the lessons God intends for us to receive, we finally open the doorway to receive inner fulfillment. Inner peace is God's signal which says, "Good, my daughter, you're now on the right track!"

The key to achieving peace is learning how to surrender. To surrender is to detach ourselves from our own expected results. We surrender when we are able to let go of our immediate desires and follow God's will. This is easier said than done! It is human nature to believe we know what's best. Therefore, we desire to stay in control. Often we do not trust the judgment of others, believing our ideals are supreme. Consequently, surrendering in many cases is not a desirable option. We don't trust people, and moreover, we even second guess our "Higher Power." Deep down inside we question, "What if God fails me?" Without faith we can do nothing! Many of us have tried everything under the sun, yet we still resort back to the same place, failure. Now it's time to try what is proven to work! Success comes when we surrender our will to God.

Many falsely believe the act of surrendering to God is all about religion; that isn't the case! Surrendering is about developing a relationship with Him. God doesn't desire us to put on a performance to please Him. He is only looking for our hearts to become open to His will for our lives. God desires us to be good people. As we renew our minds with positive thoughts and allow good to saturate our hearts, we meet God's expectancy. His will is simple; It doesn't require a lot! He simply desires that we develop a relationship built on trust in Him and live an integral lifestyle. These two prerequisites lead us to purpose, which is God's intended plan for our lives.

Our relationship with God is a "heart thing," it is not a religious duty. People wrongfully put all types of expectations and burdens on others, which is often too hard to carry, not God! He is not concerned with rituals. God is more concerned with what's inside our hearts. He wants us to be good people, not because anyone forces us, but because it's imbedded within our hearts. It is the condition of our hearts that will determine how successful we will be in life.

As we become pleasing to God, He rewards us. Peace indwells within us when God is delighted with our way of life. As we walk into purpose and do what we were created to do, God rewards us with inner fulfillment. This feeling is like no other high you can obtain in this world! Walking in our purpose feels good! The dreams and goals that God has placed within us are all part of purpose. He gives us certain desires so we will have the inner drive to achieve them. So in essence, the positive things we want to passionately achieve are generally aligned with God's will. That is why regardless of how we try to shake certain dreams or goals, the desire continues to arise.

Throughout the *Voices of Consequences Enrichment Series*, we have worked intensely to shift our focus in life. Many of us were caught up in the world's method of achieving success. In many cases, we experienced several obstacles and dilemmas because this path went against God's purpose for our lives. We now have awakened to purpose and have vigorously worked to discover just what we were created to do. We have assessed our skill sets and talents, and prayed for God to reveal what service we can do to please Him. Now that we have an outline of His desired path, we are free to walk in it! As a result, we are positioned to discover our purpose and walk in peace.

In this chapter, we will discuss the importance of peace and ways in which we can sustain it. Peace is vital for experiencing an enjoyable life! Without it, life is dark and tormenting. This chapter is essential because it will give us the road map we need to permanently destroy all areas of darkness in our lives. Absorb this vital information and implement the techniques you learn into your everyday habits.

The main ingredient many of us have lacked in our lives is peace. In many cases, life has been a constant roller coaster of ups and downs. Every time we finally think things will be fine, something else occurs. This cycle has beat many of us down and left us hopeless. We no longer have to stay in this state. Peace can become our portion! We learned peace comes when we surrender to God's will and find our purpose. We are now working hard to achieve this goal.

It is our perspective about life that helps us to sustain our peace. When obstacles arise we know they are sent to open our eyes, strengthen us, help us to change our course, and to provide a doorway to advancement. Knowing this, we are able to quickly regroup, learn our lesson, and find the growth opportunity. In turn, we pass the test! When we pass the test, the obstacle subsides and we conquer it.

We also learned the importance of delays. When they occur, generally it is a signal that we may be moving off course or speeding ahead too quickly. God uses delays to enlighten us and slow us down. Therefore, when delays occur, we now regroup, open our eyes and take heed! As we make necessary adjustments and discover God's intent for our dilemmas, we become wise and equipped! As a result, obstacles no longer beat us down; they now build us up!

We now know the importance of living an integral life. Therefore we do the right thing, all the time, whether someone is watching or not. As a result, we feel good about ourselves when we look in the mirror. Living an honorable life protects us, and enables us to avoid unnecessary shame and guilt, and walk with our head held high. Today we feel good about who we are and the things that we do. We are no longer victims to the enemy's trap of shame and guilt! We are now spiritually free!

We learned throughout the *Voices of Consequences Enrichment Series* about the importance of the mind and our thoughts. We know that all battles take place in our minds first. Therefore, we now fight our battles by changing our perspective. Today, we purposely force ourselves to see the good in every situation, so we know how to combat fear. We know fear is only false evidence appearing real, and it has no actual basis! As a result, we no longer allow events to frighten us. Instead of running away from our obstacles, we face them head on! We seek our "Higher Power" in meditation, and we discover the solution for each problem.

Trusting God gives us peace. We now know He is our Partner, our Protector, and our Friend. We know with God, we are never alone. Our trust in God brings us great security and assurance. When others are frightened and scared, we have the ability to relax. We know whatever God allows to happen will certainly work out for our good! We keep this mentality and train our minds to constantly remove all negative thoughts through meditation. Therefore, we are able to face life's obstacles fearlessly and we sustain our peace!

We have learned to develop the character trait of patience, so we know how to wait. During our waiting seasons, we utilize our time to work on "self." We sharpen our skill sets and talents on a regular basis, and we learn how to become a greater "self." As a result of our discipline, we begin to increase our self-esteem. Instead of receiving a false sense of esteem from people, places, and things, we now receive real esteem by becoming the person God created us to be. Today, we no longer look to simply please others, because we no longer seek their temporary appeasement. Our esteem now comes from within, so we are satisfied with who we are. Compliments are welcomed by people, but they are no longer necessary to survive. We now know happiness comes from within, so we no longer seek the approval of others. Instead, we create our own inner joy! Therefore, we sustain our peace.

We have learned the importance of caring for "self," so we have become our own best friend, lover, and protector. We constantly stay in tune with our needs and our desires, and we cater to "self." We do the things that make us feel good about ourselves. Today we smile as we look at ourselves in the mirror, because we realize we are indeed our own greatest asset.

We no longer allow others to hurt us or harm us. We now protect ourselves by creating boundaries. We give people the freedom to be who they are and we don't push our own agendas off on others. Today we look to people with no expectancy; therefore, they are unable to hurt us. We now know God is our Provider, so we don't look to people, places, or things for our provision. As a result, we sustain our peace.

When we experience stressful encounters with others, we look inside and ask ourselves the question, "What do I need to do to protect myself?" We learn to be kind to others, but we detach when there is potential for us to receive unjust hurt or harm. Our detachment isn't mean, nasty, or abrupt, it is loving. We give people the opportunity to get themselves together, if they choose, while we take the time we need to stop and care for "self." Therefore, we sustain our peace.

Today we no longer let people burden us with their hardships and dilemmas. We've learned that we hurt ourselves and others when we disable them by doing the things for them that they should be doing for themselves. Therefore, we are kind by showing people the solution, yet we allow them to help themselves. In addition, we don't take on other people's burdens that God doesn't intend for us to handle. As a result, we sustain our peace.

Today we no longer allow people to infect us with their negative thinking. Instead, we rid ourselves of all bad company and negativity. In exchange we surround ourselves with people who encourage us, believe in us, and promote our own advancement. When we recognize that individuals in our lives are constantly taking away, and not adding, we detach. In addition, when we see that people are distracting us from achieving our purpose, we also detach. Furthermore, when people have no desire to change and don't want to do the right things in life, we also detach. Our detachment is healthy and it helps us to sustain our peace.

Today, we no longer make decisions without counting the cost! We intensely think about our choices and measure the consequences before we act. Therefore, we refuse to over obligate ourselves. We only accept obligations that will not cause harm to "self." Therefore, we sustain our peace.

Today, before we commit to financial obligations we consider our incoming finances and our needs. We never take on financial debts that may be too difficult to pay. We allot ourselves a cushion, just in case rough times come. We live within our means, and we no longer attempt to compete with the Joneses. Instead, we take our time and acquire assets that we will keep. As a result, when it's time to pay bills we are at ease, because we have more than enough to pay our debts. Our wise choices allow us to sustain our peace.

Our obstacles have taught us what is important in life. Therefore, people, places, and things are no longer our idols, so we don't waste our time and efforts seeking fulfillment from them. Instead, we learn how to budget our time wisely, and we prioritize developing our relationship with God. As a result, we sustain our peace.

In addition, we prioritize the attention of our loved ones. We enjoy being immersed in their love, so we show them our gratitude. We recognize from our dilemmas the ones who love us and will stand by us. Therefore, we honor those who have given us their support. We make them feel good about themselves through our loving, kind actions, and we promote their endeavors. In turn, they do the same for us. Therefore, we sustain our peace.

When life becomes overwhelming, we know what to do. We have learned techniques on how to maintain our joy. As a result, we are equipped to handle whatever dilemmas may come our way. We are empowered to overcome. Therefore, we sustain our peace.

Today, we know, no man can give us peace. It is a gift from God. He sends peace to our minds through our thoughts. As we take control over our minds, we win every battle, and learn how to tear down every negative thought that would try and attack us. As we rid ourselves of negativity and all negative thoughts, we achieve peace!

Peace comes with learning how to properly perceive the events of life. As we gain knowledge we are enlightened. A problem isn't a problem at all, if we know how to fix it. Dilemmas no longer disturb us when we know the direction to take to overcome them. As we work on "self," and spend time with our "Higher Power," we receive revelations. This enlightenment will take us places in life we never dreamed we could go!

A large part of our interactions on earth are done with people. Therefore, in order to sustain our peace, we must master interpersonal relations with others. We cannot allow people to steal our joy. Maintaining peace is learning how to become a peacemaker on earth. Instead of fueling fires, we learn how to put them out. We diffuse arguments by being kind and refusing to take part in them. As a result, we become a voice of reason that exposes the truth. Today, we learn to consider others and their feelings. We don't say or do things that may be offensive. We give people the freedom of expression and allow them to be who they are. Instead of promoting discord, we promote peace. As a result, we learn how to rise above adversity and allow God to use us by becoming a peacemaker.

Today we are no longer the same. We are at ease and feel good about our accomplishments. We've learned the secret to success and a good life, and have what many others lack. We have peace!

Now we understand the importance of obtaining and maintaining peace, let's take a look at some examples that will illuminate the strategies of how we can sustain peace throughout our journey of life.

EXAMPLE 1-

Judith worked as a bank teller in Atlanta, Georgia to pay her way through college. She was a hard worker who was raised by two strict parents, which she obtained guidance from. One day Judith was convinced by one of her friends to go out to a night club to party. She accepted the invitation and met a boy named Frank from College Park, Georgia. Frank was a thug who robbed people for a living, but Judith didn't know it. She was attracted to his nice smile and his swagger.

Frank began to spend a lot of time with Judith, and she fell in love with him. Shortly after, she began skipping classes and missing work to hang out with him in College Park.

One day, Frank convinced Judith to help him set up the bank she worked at to be robbed. Judith didn't want to do it, but Frank's pressure became more intense. Reluctantly, she

155

agreed to give Frank the inside information he needed to pull off his heist, and the plan went into effect.

With Judith's help, Frank and his boys robbed the bank and made off with over $350,000 in cash. Frank was extremely delighted with his new come up. Both Judith and Frank enjoyed their new life of luxury, spending the money gained from the robbery.

Shortly after, one of the boys who assisted in the robbery began to brag about their success to a man who was an informant. The informant lured the boy to talk more about the robbery on a wire. As a result, the police were able to link all of the participants back to the crime, including Judith. Consequently, they were all charged and arrested for bank robbery.

Judith's parents were devastated! They quickly bailed their daughter out of jail. For months Judith remained in fear, awaiting her sentencing. Every day she would ponder on thoughts about prison that would frighten her. As a result, she had no peace.

Judith's sentencing day finally arrived. After spending thousands of dollars in legal fees, her lawyer was able to get her a twenty four month sentence in Federal Prison, rather than a ten year sentence that was originally offered.

Even though Judith made out well, she couldn't see herself surviving in prison. She had a short amount of time to prepare. Judith was allowed to self-surrender, three weeks after sentencing. Nervous and extremely scared, she dreadfully prepared to go to prison, and her parents helped her get through it.

Judith self-surrendered to Tallahassee Federal Correctional Institution, where she was greeted by several of the female inmates. After the first two weeks, Judith became a little more at peace. She realized her time was nothing compared to the fate of so many others she came in contact with.

Judith enrolled in college courses and finished where she left off. She also got heavily involved with the Christian Prison Ministry where she began to gain more strength. As Judith reconciled her relationship with her "Higher Power," she began to receive peace in her mind and her heart. Judith recognized her shortcomings and took steps to change her life. She utilized her time in prison to work on "self." She dealt with her issues of low self-esteem, fear, worry and doubt. As a result, Judith became a better person.

Today Judith is out of prison and living a great life! She goes to the local jail once a week as a partner in a prison ministry. She teaches the girls the techniques she learned to receive peace and restoration. She just finished college and is engaged to a successful dentist. Judith has vowed to live life on the right track this time around. Her integral lifestyle helps her to maintain her peace.

EXAMPLE TWO-

Sabrina came home from prison and got a part time job at Checkers to get back on her feet. Sabrina also signed up for classes at the local community college. As a result, she got back on her feet and was doing well.

One day she went to her cousin's cookout and linked up with some of her old friends, who were happy to see her. Sabrina exchanged numbers with her old friend Sara and the two of them stayed in touch.

Every time Sabrina began to study, Sara would call her cell phone. Sabrina loved Sara, so she would entertain her calls. Sabrina stopped her studies and started hanging out late with her. Sara began to tell Sabrina how useless college was. She also insulted Sabrina telling her that she was an ex-convict and no one would ever hire her except a fast food spot like Checkers.

Deep down inside Sara was jealous of Sabrina. She had seen how well Sabrina was doing in such a short time and wanted to take her off her course. Sara hadn't been to prison, but never made any substantial accomplishments. Her life was consumed with partying, men and drugs.

Sabrina stayed down with Sara, but her constant insults began to get to Sabrina. Consequently, Sabrina's grades suffered and she almost lost her job at Checkers when her boss saw her giving away extra food to Sara and her friends. Sabrina got called into the boss's office and he threatened to fire her if she didn't get her act together. Sabrina's boss had mercy on her because he believed in her. His faith sparked her to turn her life back around.

Sabrina realized when Sara came around she lost her discipline, and her overall peace. Therefore, she decided it was time to detach from Sara. After she let her go, things began to get much better. Sabrina started to take back control over her life and did the things that were necessary for her to succeed.

With hard work and diligence, Sabrina graduated community college and is now the manager of Checkers. She is also back in school, where she is studying to receive her Bachelor's degree in Business Administration. She has great goals and plans in life, and she is determined to reach them!

Are you ready to take back your peace? You don't have to live in fear or torment anymore! If you are ready for change, follow me in this prayer: *"God, I thank You for showing me the importance of peace and a sound mind. Help me to take control over my thoughts and rid myself of all negative thinking. Allow*

Your perfect love to rid me of all fear, worry, and doubt. Help me to recognize the things in my life that hinder my peace and give me the strength to detach from them. Help me manage my time and do things that are useful and productive. Give me a voice of reason that tears down all arguments, confusion and dissention. Lead me with Your divine direction, so I will do the things that will help me maintain my peace. Help me to stay focused on You and Your perfect plan for my life. I thank You for the character trait of peace. I now take it on as my own. Amen."

Congratulations! You have taken another huge step in your pursuit to a great "self." With your character trait of peace, you can be calm and serene, even in the midst of a storm. This character trait will take you to great levels in life. May peace always be with you!

QUESTIONS-

1) What is peace?
2) Why is remaining peaceful important?
3) How do we sustain our peace?
4) In what ways might people become a distraction to us?
5) How do we prevent distractions?
6) Why are our thoughts so important in maintaining peace?

WRITING ASSIGNMENT-

Write out an affirmation of the things you can do each day that will help you sustain your peace.

CHAPTER 12
Making Integrity a Lifestyle

We have reached the end of the journey in our pursuit to become a greater "self." We now realize that our behavior and moral standards determine the quality of our lives. As we change our way of thinking and improve our character defects, we can reach unimaginable heights of achievement! We now know that it is our character that will protect us from making wrong choices. Therefore, we have developed high moral standards, which have prepared us to soar in life!

In this book, we learned to develop eleven important character traits. These traits include: love, honesty, loyalty, humility and contentment, generosity, joy and a good attitude, trustworthiness and dependability, patience, kindness, self-control, and peace. These character traits are essential in helping us to achieve restoration.

This book is not to be read once and then discarded. Study it and let it be your study guide, which serves as a map to your new abundant life. Review this text during your daily meditation and find new ways to develop the character traits enclosed. Become conscious of your behavior, and check to see if you are living up to the moral standards of good character. When necessary make adjustments in the areas you need to fix.

Living an honorable lifestyle will not necessarily be easy, nor will it happen overnight. It may take hard work to get on track and reach your desired results. If you fall short, it's okay. Dust yourself off and begin again! We are human beings. No one is faultless; nor are we expected to be. All that is required is an open heart, which is willing to change. What we cannot achieve in our own strength, God will help us achieve. Continue to study and read this book until the information enclosed is imbedded in your heart and your character shines brightly. Examine your changes and record them. Write down the differences you observe in your *Voices of Consequences Enrichment Series, A Pursuit to a Greater "Self" Workbook/Journal*. As you write down your progress, it will help you clearly recognize how far you have come and how many improvements you need to make.

Now let's explore some affirmations that illustrate the new character traits we have developed. You can use them in your time of daily meditation. Say them out loud with meaning, and let the words become one with your heart. You will be amazed how what you speak will turn into your reality. Expect great changes! Success is just ahead!

1) **Love-** Love is the most powerful force in the universe. It has the ability to pierce the hearts of others. It is the basis of integrity and all of our character traits are derived from it. Without love we have nothing! Love is essential for every form of real success. Therefore, we open our hearts to be saturated with love, so we have victory!

    Love is patient and love is kind. It has no hidden motives, nor does it hurt. It recognizes the needs of others and performs on their behalf. Real love is genuine and sincere. It looks for nothing in return. Its purity can easily be spotted and becomes contagious to all whom it comes in contact with. Love lives within our hearts and when ignited it becomes one with us. As we spend time with our "Higher Power," our love for humanity increases. We learn to love others with the same agape love that God gives us. As a result, our love becomes an act of service and honor to God. When we express our love to others, God in return reinforces His loves to us.

2) **Honesty**- Honesty is the standard we live by. We make it our priority to always tell the truth. We are truthful with ourselves, just as we are with others. Therefore, we no longer live in denial. We are now able to openly recognize our shortcomings and we fix them. We no longer wear masks of deception, which once hindered us and held us bound. Instead, we remove our mask and make necessary changes, until we are able to be happy with "self."

Today, we no longer intentionally deceive or mislead others. Instead, we are honest and when we are wrong we accept responsibility for our actions. As a result, we no longer tell lies to cover up the wrong we have done. Instead, we accept our mistakes and we make necessary adjustments to fix them.

Today, we no longer tell lies to appease those around us. Instead, we present ourselves to be who we truly are. We allow others the choice to accept us, if they choose. If not, it's okay, because we are content with ourselves and we do not need the gratification of others. Instead of seeking praise from man, our goal is to seek God's recognition and approval.

Today, we are honest in our actions. We no longer compromise our integrity by doing things we know we should not do. We know compromise is the greatest trap for self-destruction. Therefore, we avoid compromising behavior at all costs! We now realize whatever we obtain on false pretenses, or through short-cuts, will ultimately be taken away. In addition, we realize short-cuts aren't short-cuts at all; they lead back to one place, the beginning. Therefore, we are honest in all of our dealings.

Today, we know the only way to truly live abundantly is by being honest in all aspects of our life, therefore we set our moral standards with a bar of honesty. As a result, we are honest with ourselves and others, and we are honest in all of our dealings.

3) **Loyalty**- Loyalty is the foundation of every solid relationship. Our loyalty creates trust in the heart of others. It also builds a wall of protection around those whom we are loyal to. Today, we no longer join in slander with others. Instead, we stand up and protect our neighbors from harm, and display our loyalty.

Loyalty is built without self-interest in mind. We stand loyal as an expression of our unconditional love. As a result, our loyalty is given without any expectancy in return. It is done because we know it is the right thing to do.

We've learned in this journey our first commitment of loyalty is to God. We know He gives us life and provides all of our needs. Therefore, we remain loyal to God in all of our dealings. We take the time out to commune with Him daily in prayer and meditation. We surrender our will and pick up His desired plan for our lives. Therefore, we constantly analyze our actions and our motives to make sure we stay in the will of God. We live integral lives as our service or offering to Him. Today, our goal is to please God in all our dealings, so we are protected from the wiles of evil and deception. We also receive the prize of good, peaceful living, which is our reward from God for doing the right thing.

Our loyalty to God is our protection from evil and hidden motives. We train ourselves to be loyal and to have integrity, regardless of our circumstances and situations, so we no longer compromise our integrity and we no longer waver!

4) **Humility and Contentment**- Life's obstacles have shown us the need to always remain humble. Despite the achievements we accomplish, we do not become boastful or proud. Instead, we become grateful. We recognize God as our Provider. All good things are possible only because of Him. Therefore, we do not let success and the praise of others go to our heads. Today, we realize that as quickly as people build us up, any wrong move will cause them to tear us down. Knowing this, we don't look to people for praise or esteem. Instead, we look to God. He is our rewarder!

In all our dealings, we remain humble. We treat all our fellow neighbors the same, regardless of who they are. We recognize the fact that we are not better than anyone; it's only our honorable actions and correct choices that open the doors for more blessings. Therefore, we don't get caught up in the pleasures of the world and we don't rely on false idols for fulfillment. We now know external things only bring about temporary happiness. Therefore, we get caught up in pleasing God and we are purpose driven. As a result, we are motivated to do the very things we were placed on this earth to accomplish.

Today, we are no longer distracted by material things or fast money. We recognize they are a set up, and true fulfillment only comes from within. Therefore, we become content with who we are and the things that we have. We no longer try and compete with the Joneses; nor are we jealous of others. We recognize our ability to improve "self," and we do the necessary work to achieve our own goals. Therefore, we are content and happy with "self."

Today, we are no longer stubborn; our hearts are open to change. We realize we don't have all the answers, and we don't know everything. Therefore, we are open to wisdom and knowledge. We delight in the opportunity to learn more. We listen to the good advice of others who have wisdom. When we are corrected because of our wrong doings, we humble ourselves and receive the guidance we need with a grateful attitude. We acknowledge our faults and do what is necessary to fix them. Today, we always remain humble, regardless of our measure of success, so we are empowered!

5) **Generosity**- Today, we hold the trait of generosity, which unlocks the doorway to our prosperity and provisions. Each day we arise, we think about how we can be a blessing. As a result, giving has become a natural habit. It is what we do as our service to God.

Today, we contently seek ways that we can give to others who are less fortunate than we are. As a result, we are God's vessels whom He uses to funnel gifts to His children. As we come more into alignment with God, we become His partner, and He richly blesses us. As we show our generosity, we feel joy and fulfillment inside, because we are doing the very things we were put on this planet to accomplish.

Today, our giving is done out of love and a pure heart, so we have no hidden motives. As a result, our actions are deeply felt by others, who immediately recognize the depth of our sincerity. As we give to people, their hearts are enlightened and they are transformed by our love. Because of its power, our giving becomes contagious, and others delight in joining in. As a result, we start a flame of love in our cycle of giving.

As we delight in our generosity, we actively take into account just what we can give. Today, we know we can give our time, our money, our skill sets and talents, and our service. We assess the needs of others as God leads us. We give what we can afford, yet, at the same time, we care for "self." Even in our giving, we never do things that will harm our well-being. We are strictly led by God.

Today, we show our generosity by empowering others, so we don't allow our giving to disable them. We don't do for others the things they should be doing for themselves. We make sure our gifts don't block the advancement of people. Therefore, we give lovingly, helping those who are willing to help themselves. As a result, our generosity builds our neighbors up; it does not tear them down!

Our generosity allows our recipients freedom of choice. We do not push our agenda on others. Our giving is with no strings attached. We allow people to grow in their own timing. In our giving, we expect no payment in return, nor do we have any expectations on recipients. Therefore, we are never disappointed by the reaction of others. We now realize that only God can change their hearts, so we no longer attempt to change people. Instead of trying to manipulate others by our actions, we now know how to carry our concerns to God in our time of daily prayer. What we cannot do, we know God can do!

Today, we become a help to those who encounter hardships, by asking God to intervene. Our intercession provokes Him to act and circumstances change by the power of His love. Therefore, we are caught up in doing the things that bring pleasure to God. Today, we serve God to the best of our ability with the gift of generosity!

6) **The Strength of Joy and a Good Attitude**- We welcome each day with an attitude of gratitude. Therefore, we know good things will happen this day. We do not let the adversities of life weigh down on us or tear us apart. Instead, we purposely look for the good in every situation. As a result, we are always able to sustain our peace.

Today, we live life with expectancy of great things to come. Therefore, we immerse ourselves with thoughts of peace, joy, and happiness. We let our minds and hearts become saturated with our positive thoughts, which allow us to maintain an attitude of joy.

Today, we are no longer hindered by fear. We now know fear is only: false evidence appearing real. Therefore, we are not frightened by its power. Instead, we immediately dethrone every fearful thought that comes into our minds by taking it to God in meditation. We now rid of ourselves of negative thoughts and replace them with positive thoughts. Therefore, our positivity wins the battle over all negativity. As a result, negative things are no longer allowed to penetrate. Before they form, we demolish them with positive thoughts, so we maintain our joy!

Today, we realize obstacles are sent to make us better, so we no longer run or hide from them. Instead, we take on challenges head on and we embrace them. We joyfully seek out the opportunities to make us stronger. Therefore, we remain joyful when others become scared and frightened. Today, we possess the information to overcome any obstacle that comes our way, so we are not moved! Knowing what to do brings us peace. Therefore, we remain joyful.

Today, we no longer look to false idols, to create our happiness. We now know happiness only comes from within. Therefore, we take out the time to learn more about ourselves, so we are now equipped with the ability to tap into our inner joy at any time. Today, we know the things to do to care for "self." Therefore, we have become stewards of our happiness. As a result, we walk in line with God's purpose. We fulfill our assignments here on earth, as we maintain our joy.

Today, we recognize the power of our own personal energy, so we always greet our neighbors with an attitude of joy and gratitude. Even when others are mean and harsh, we keep our character intact. Our sincere actions become the knife that convicts the hearts of others, and sparks them to do the right thing. We know gratitude and kindness can overcome any form of evil, and keep us calm and peaceful at the same time. Therefore, we are empowered with the secret weapon that helps us maintain our joy!

7) Trustworthiness and Dependability- Today, we are individuals who are trustworthy and dependable. Therefore, people are proud to call us their friends, partners, and employees. We are reliable and prompt to answer the call of duty, and we prioritize the needs of others.

Today, we honor our words of commitment. We fulfill our obligations at the time we commit to do them. As a result, our sincere actions brightly shine forth and display our true character. We no longer make promises to others, without first counting the cost. Instead, we think through our actions before we speak, weighing out the pros and cons. We never make obligations that will compromise our care for "self." We make commitments to only do the things that are in our strength and power to do, and we do not over commit to anyone. We prioritize our health and our peace of mind, so we plan our lives accordingly. We allot enough time to take care of each matter on our daily agenda, and we allow extra time for incidentals. Therefore, we no longer over obligate ourselves to people or assignments that will take us of our track. Instead, we count the cost first, and commit ourselves to what we can do comfortably. As a result, we are trustworthy and dependable.

In this journey of life, we've learned how to become great starters as well as great finishers. We've learned to pace ourselves and maintain our persistence, so we successfully complete our tasks. We adopt the motto, "quitting isn't an option," so we finish our course with pride and joy. When things get difficult, we pray to God for strength, regroup, and focus our energy on what we need to do to sustain. In addition, we reach out for help when we run into difficulties. We never let pride get in our way to success. Even when we are tired, we dig within and muster up the energy we need to persevere. As a result, we are known to others as trustworthy and reliable.

8) **Patience**- We have learned that life primarily consists of the process of waiting for something. Everything good that comes, happens in a certain season. Knowing this truth, we've learned that we need patience to succeed. Our patience is the ability to wait at ease, without becoming anxious, frustrated, or discouraged. To conquer patience, we've learned how to become productive in our periods of delay. Today, we realize delays are sent from God. It is His way of saying, "Yes, I will make it happen, but just not now." We also know delays are sent to help us prepare for what we are anticipating. Therefore, during our season of delay, we don't just twiddle our thumbs. Instead, we utilize delays to work on "self."

Today, we recognize delays for what they are. They are often God-sent "time-outs." He allows delays so we can take a break to prepare for the next phase of life. Knowing this truth, we embrace these seasons and utilize the extra time we are given productively. As a result, it is in our season of delays that we become better people.

Today, when obstacles occur, we no longer complain or grumble. Instead, we seek God and see what He is trying to tell us. We know that all things will work out for our good, so we program our minds to always recognize the opportunity that can come from whatever situations we may experience.

We know now, we have the power to label our experience. If we label it good, we will see the benefit that it will bring. If we label it bad, we can expect it to be just that. Therefore, we take power over our dilemmas by always labeling them correctly. Our perspective gives us peace and makes it easier to wait with patience.

Today, we recognize all short-cuts taken in life only have one result—failure. Therefore, we take our time and get through each step and phase of life. We no longer rush to get to the finish line. Instead, we pace ourselves, with ease. As a result, we build our lives on a solid foundation, doing things the right way the first time around. Therefore, we no longer have to look over our shoulder, and the things we obtain we are able to keep. Our avoidance of short-cuts helps us stay at peace. As a result, we have patience that helps us rule in life!

9) **Kindness**- Our journey has taught us to be vessels full of love. Therefore, we are kind to our neighbors. We treat people with care and compassion and we look out for the best interest of our neighbors, as we care for "self."

Today, we are honorable people, who have patience with others. We are gentle, kind, & understanding, which causes us to be sought out as friends. We are merciful and forgiving, despite what others do in return. We know the power of our kindness, so we use it as our chosen weapon of defense. When others are nasty, harsh and bitter to us, we repay them with our kindness. Our soft, gentle words pierce through them like a knife. As a result, through our acts of kindness, our foes become our friends.

Today, our kindness causes us to respect and appreciate others. We honor those who have authority over us by performing their wishes with a good attitude. We also respect those who we encounter throughout the day. We monitor our tones of expression when we speak, and we consider the feelings of others. Instead of ripping people down with our words, we encourage our neighbors and we build them up. Our kindness is done out of our hearts, with no expectancy in return. We are kind simply because it is the right thing to do. It is an act of service to God that we perform proudly.

As we are kind to others, we take into consideration our own needs. We don't neglect "self," to please or satisfy someone else. We care for ourselves, as we consider the needs of others. We don't impose our agenda on people. Instead, we allow them to do what they need to do in order to care for themselves. As a result, we are no longer care-takers of people. We let everyone do for themselves the things they need to do to become productive, responsible people. As a result, our kindness is no longer taken for weakness. We now set boundaries that protect us being taken advantage of.

Today, when it is necessary to protect ourselves, we know how to detach. Our detachment is done in a loving, kind manner, in order to give ourselves and others the freedom to grow.

Today, we no longer hold on to anger and resentment. We now realize who our true enemy is. Therefore, we understand when people are ignorant to the devices of the enemy, they are vulnerable to be used. We take this knowledge into account when others do us harm. Therefore, we do not hang on to bitterness. Instead, we forgive our enemies, even when it is difficult to do. By forgiving them, we unhook the handcuffs that locked us to the pain they inflicted upon us. As a result, we remain free.

Today, we have a new nature. We possess a loving heart that is kind!

10) **Self-Control**- Today, we are rulers over our lives because we have self-control. We no longer act solely based on our feelings or emotions. Instead, we think before we react. We measure the consequences for our actions and we don't put our lives in jeopardy to take revenge. Today, when things get to difficult for us to bear, we detach ourselves and seek God.

As a result, we allow Him to handle all of the things we cannot handle in our own strength, and we are victorious!

Today, we recognize, we cannot control people no matter how hard we try. Even if we inflict pain on others, after the pain is over, they will still remain the same. Only God has the ability to change the hearts of people, so we go to God in prayer. He gives us the strength and the ability to remain calm and endure. At the same time, he touches the heart of the person we bring to Him in prayer. We are empowered, because we know how to seek God and allow him to be our Avenger.

Today, we are rulers because we know how to control our thoughts. We no longer allow negativity to sink into our minds. Instead, we constantly dethrone all negative thoughts. As a result, we control our actions by controlling our minds.

Today, we use meditation as a way of constantly ridding our minds of all negativity. As a result, our minds are renewed and our thoughts remain pure. Through meditation, we have learned to master our emotions. We no longer let negative feelings linger within us. Instead, we deal with the root of our problems and discard all negative thoughts. Therefore, we have self- control. We don't let situations control us; we now hold the ability to control them!

We no longer allow others to push our buttons based on what they say or what they do. We are no longer moved by what people think about us. Instead, we are focused on living by God's standards. Therefore, we are no longer people pleasers. We do the right thing as our act of service to God, and we no longer look to others for provisions. Therefore, people can no longer disappoint us. As a result, we are deeply rooted in our relationship with our "Higher Power." Therefore, we maintain our self-control.

11) **Peace**- Today, we are empowered by our character trait of peace. We no longer waste our efforts in attempts to wrestle with God. Today, we surrender our own will and seek the will of God, so when others struggle we have peace.

We now realize all circumstances we encounter are allowed by God. We see obstacles for what they are—an opportunity to advance. Therefore, we search intensely for the good they can produce, so we make the best out of all situations. Knowing good things will ultimately manifest, we are able to maintain our peace.

When things don't happen as we plan, we don't get frightened or frustrated. We now have the ability to carry all of our problems and burdens to God in prayer. Because He is our Problem Solver, we sustain our peace.

Today, we live an honorable life. We do the right things, all the time, whether someone is watching or not. As a result, we no longer have to look over our shoulders or behind our backs because of our adverse actions. Instead, we maintain our peace.

Today, when we stare in the mirror, we feel good about ourselves. We now recognize our potential and see the progress we've made. We no longer have to walk in mediocrity, or below the standards of others. We now value ourselves, so daily we strive to walk in our purpose.

Our obstacles have taught us what we are made of. We now know we are not weak. Today, we are strong, like eagles that soar high! We recognize our flaws and have made the necessary adjustments. Each day, we make it a priority to become a better "self." We are proud of our achievements. Therefore, we sustain our peace!

This has been a long journey, but we have finally arrived! Today, we have tapped into our greater "self." This book holds the key ingredients as to what we must strive to maintain in order to sustain a good life. If we live life by these standards, we can sustain the success we obtain. Without character, we are open to the traps of self-destruction. Therefore, we need integrity to build a fence of protection around us and keep us out of dark places.

I believe we all can agree; prison is not a place where we want to return. We don't have to! Today, we have the ability to soar! True success comes when our talent matches up to our character. As we become honorable people, our potential in life becomes endless. We can become whatever we desire. Life does not end here. Prison wasn't sent to destroy us; this trip occurred to wake us up! You now hold the road map to success in your hands. You have all the ingredients you need to bake the cake!

Congratulations. You finally arrived in your pursuit to a greater "self." You have earned your wings; the only thing left to do is fly. What are you waiting for? Spread your wings and soar!

QUESTIONS

1) Why is developing good character traits important?
2) How can you work on developing your character?
3) Name the 11 positive character traits we learned about in our pursuit to a greater "self?'
4) What is the most important character trait out of all 11 character traits? Why?
5) How can you continue to use this book to help you develop good character?
6) What character trait seems to be the most difficult for you to establish? Why?

WRITING ASSIGNMENT

Action Step:

Write out all eleven character traits we discussed in this book. Write a paragraph to describe each character trait and what it means to you. Then write out what you personally can do to incorporate each trait into your life.

REFERENCES

CHAPTER ONE

The New King James Version Bible, Nashville, Tennessee:
Thomas Nelson Inc., 1982.

Casarjian, Robin. *House of Healing*. Boston: Lionheart
Press, 1995.

Meyer, Joyce. *Battlefield of The Mind*. New York: Hachette
Book Company USA, 1995.

Warren, Rick. *The Purpose Driven Life*. Zondervan, 2002.

Williamson, Marianne. A *Return to Love*. New York: Harper
Collins Publishers, 1992.

CHAPTER TWO

The New King James Version Bible, Nashville, Tennessee:
Thomas Nelson Inc., 1982.

Meyer, Joyce. *Battlefield of The Mind*. New York: Hachette
Book Company USA, 1995.

Peale, Norman Vincent. *The Power of Positive Thinking*.
Prentice Hall, 1996.

CHAPTER THREE

Allen, James. *As A Man Thinketh*. Raddord, VA: Wilder
Publications, 2007.

Byrne, Rhonda. *The Secret*. New York: Atria Books, 2006.

The New King James Version Bible, Nashville, Tennessee:
Thomas Nelson Inc., 1982.

Jordan, Bernard. *The Laws of Thinking.* Hay House, 2006.
Meyer, Joyce. *Battlefield of The Mind.* New York: Hachette
   Book Company USA, 1995.
Peale, Norman Vincent. *The Power of Positive Thinking.*
   Prentice Hall, 1996.
Williamson, Marianne. *A Return to Love.* New York: Harper
   Collins Publishers, 1992.

CHAPTER FOUR

The New King James Version Bible, Nashville, Tennessee:
   Thomas Nelson Inc., 1982.
Warren, Rick. *The Purpose Driven Life.* Zondervan, 2002.

CHAPTER FIVE

Canfield, Jack. Hansen, Mark and Hewitt, Les. *The Power
   of Focus.* Deerfield Beach Florida: Peale, Health
   Communications Inc., 2000.
Hill, Napoleon. *Think and Grow Rich.* Capstone, 2009.

CHAPTER SIX

Canfield, Jack. Hansen, Mark and Hewitt, Les. *The Power
   of Focus.* Deerfield Beach Florida: Peale, Health
   Communications Inc., 2000
Hill, Napoleon. *Think and Grow Rich.* Capstone, 2009.

CHAPTER SEVEN

The New King James Version Bible, Nashville, Tennessee:
   Thomas Nelson Inc., 1982.
Byrne, Rhonda. *The Secret.* New York: Atria Books, 2006.
Hill, Napoleon. *Think and Grow Rich.* Capstone, 2009.
Jordan, Bernard. *The Laws of Thinking.* Hay House, 2006.

Meyer, Joyce. *Battlefield of The Mind*. New York: Hachette
    Book Company USA, 1995.
Peale, Norman. Vincent. *The Power of Positive Thinking*.
    Prentice Hall, 1996.
Warren, Rick. *The Purpose Driven Life*. Zondervan, 2002.

CHAPTER EIGHT

The New King James Version Bible, Nashville, Tennessee:
    Thomas Nelson Inc., 1982.
Hill, Napoleon. *Think and Grow Rich*. Capstone, 2009.
Simmons, Russell. *Do You*. New York: Gotham Books, 2007.

CHAPTER NINE

Allen, James. *As A Man Thinketh*, Raddord, VA: Wilder
    Publications, 2007.
Byrne, Rhonda. *The Secret*. New York: Atria Books, 2006.
The New King James Version Bible, Nashville, Tennessee:
    Thomas Nelson Inc, 1982.
Hill, Napoleon. *Think and Grow Rich*. Capstone, 2009.
Peale, Norman Vincent, *The Power of Positive Thinking*.
    Prentice Hall, 1996.
Simmons, Russell. *Do You*. New York: Gotham Books, 2007.

CHAPTER TEN

The New King James Version Bible, Nashville, Tennessee:
    Thomas Nelson Inc, 1982.
Canfield, Jack. Hansen, Mark and Hewitt, Les. *The Power
    of Focus*. Deerfield Beach Florida: Peale, Health
    Communications Inc., 2006.
Warren, Rick. *The Purpose Driven Life*. Zondervan, 2002.

CHAPTER ELEVEN

Canfield, Jack. Hansen, Mark and Hewitt, Les. *The Power of Focus*. Deerfield Beach Florida: Peale, Health Communications Inc., 2006.

Hill, Napoleon. *Think and Grow Rich*. Capstone, 2009.

CHAPTER TWELVE

The New King James Version Bible, Nashville, Tennessee: Thomas Nelson Inc., 1982.

Byrne, Rhonda. *The Secret*. New York: Atria Books, 2006.

Jordan, Bernard. *The Laws of Thinking*. Hay House, 2006.

Peale, Norman Vincent. *The Power of Positive Thinking*. Prentice Hall, 1996.

Williamson, Marianne. *A Return to Love*. New York: Harper Collins Publishers, 1992.

About the Author

J amila T. Davis, born and raised in Jamaica Queens, New York, is a motivational speaker and the creator of the Voices of Consequences Enrichment Series for incarcerated women. Through her powerful delivery, Davis illustrates the real-life lessons and consequences that result from poor choices. She also provides the techniques and strategies that she personally has utilized to dethrone negative thinking patterns, achieve emotional healing, and restoration and growth. Davis is no stranger to triumphs and defeats. By the age of 25, she utilized her business savvy and street smarts to rise to the top of her field, becoming a lead go-to-person in the Hip-Hop Music Industry and a self-made millionaire through real estate investments. Davis lived a care-free lavish lifestyle, surrounded by rap stars, professional sports figures and other well known celebrities.

All seemed well until the thorn of materialism clouded Davis' judgments and her business shortcuts backfired, causing her self-made empire to crumble. Davis was convicted of bank fraud, for her role in a multi-million dollar bank fraud scheme, and sentenced to 12 1/2 years in federal prison.

Davis' life was in a great shambles as she faced the obstacle of imprisonment. While living in a prison cell, stripped of all her worldly possessions, and abandoned by most of her peers, she was forced to deal with the root of her dilemmas- her own inner self.

Davis searched passionately for answers and strategies to heal and regain her self-confidence, and to discover her life's purpose. She utilized her formal training from Lincoln University, in Philadelphia, Pennsylvania, Associate Degree in Psychology, BA in Christian Education, Newburgh Seminary along with her real-life post-incarceration experiences and documented her discoveries. Revealing the tools, techniques and strategies she used to heal, Davis composed a series of books geared to empower women. Davis' goal is to utilize her life experiences to uplift, inspire and empower her audience to achieve spiritual and emotional wholeness and become their very best, despite their dilemmas and past obstacles.

Voices International Publications Presents

$\mathcal{V}oices_{of}$
CONSEQUENCES
ENRICHMENT SERIES
CREATED BY: JAMILA T. DAVIS

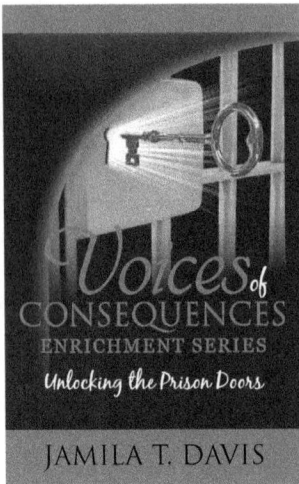

Unlocking the Prison Doors: 12 Points to Inner Healing and Restoration

ISBN: 978-09855807-4-2 Textbook
ISBN: 978-09855807-5-9 Workbook/Journal
ISBN: 978-09855807-6-6 Curriculum Guide

Unlocking the Prison Doors is a nondenominational, faith-based instructional manual created to help incarcerated women gain inner healing and restoration. In a comforting voice that readers can recognize and understand, this book provides the tools women need to get past the stage of denial and honestly assess their past behavioral patterns, their criminal conduct and its impact on their lives and others. It provides a platform for women to begin a journey of self-discovery, allowing them to assess the root of their problems and dilemmas and learn how to overcome them.

This book reveals real-life examples and concrete strategies that inspire women to release anger, fear, shame and guilt and embrace a new world of opportunities.

After reading *Unlocking the Prison Doors,* readers will be empowered to release the inner shackles and chains that have been holding them bound and begin to soar in life!

UOICES
INTERNATIONAL PUBLICATIONS
"Changing Lives One Page At A Time."
www.vocseries.com

Voices International Publications Presents

$\mathcal{V}oices_{of}$
CONSEQUENCES
ENRICHMENT SERIES
CREATED BY: JAMILA T. DAVIS

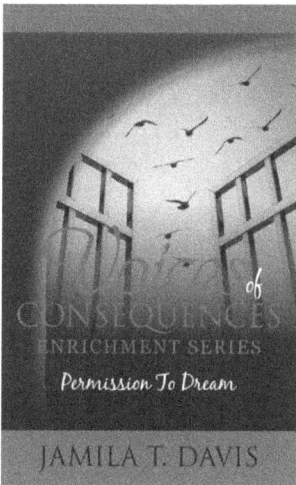

**Permission to Dream:
12 Points to Discovering Your
Life's Purpose and Recapturing
Your Dreams**

ISBN: 978-09855807-4-2 Textbook
ISBN: 978-09855807-5-9 Workbook/Journal
ISBN: 978-09855807-6-6 Curriculum Guide

Permission to Dream is a nondenominational, faith-based, instruction manual created to inspire incarcerated women to discover their purpose in life and recapture their dreams. In a way readers can identify with and understand, this book provides strategies they can use to overcome the stigma and barriers of being an ex-felon.

This book reveals universal laws and proven self-help techniques that successful people apply in their everyday lives. It helps readers identify and destroy bad habits and criminal thinking patterns, enabling them to erase the defilement of their past.

Step-by-step this book empowers readers to recognize their talents and special skill sets, propelling them to tap into the power of "self" and discover their true potential, and recapture their dreams.

After reading *Permission To Dream*, readers will be equipped with courage and tenacity to take hold of their dreams and become their very best!

UOICES
INTERNATIONAL PUBLICATIONS
"Changing Lives One Page At A Time."
www.vocseries.com

Voices International Publications Presents

$\mathcal{V}oices_{of}$
CONSEQUENCES
ENRICHMENT SERIES
CREATED BY: JAMILA T. DAVIS

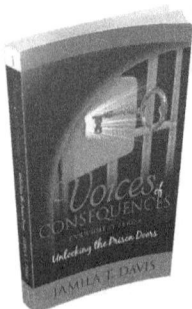

Volume #1-
Unlocking the
Prison Doors:
12 Points to Inner
Healing and
Restoration
ISBN: 978-09855807-0-4

Volume #2-
Permission
to Dream:
12 Points to Recapturing
Your Dreams and
Discovering Your
Life's Purpose
ISBN: 978-09855807-4-2

Volume #3-
Pursuit To A Greater "Self:"
12 Points to Developing Good
Character Traits and Healthy
Relationships
ISBN: 978-09855807-7-3

Purchase your copies today!
Visit us on the web @ www.vocseries.com, or write us at
196-03 Linden Blvd. St. Albans, NY 11412

VOICES
INTERNATIONAL PUBLICATIONS
"Changing Lives One Page At A Time."

"Every negative choice we make in life comes with a consequence. Sometimes the costs we are forced to pay are severe!"
— Jamila T. Davis

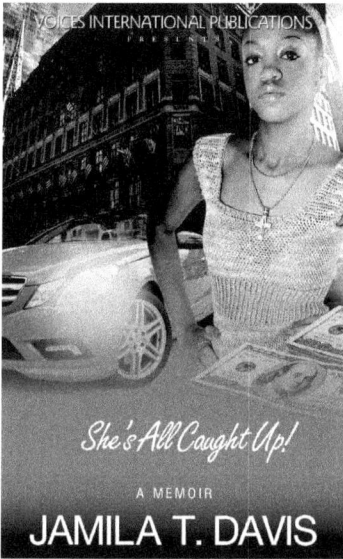

She's All Caught Up is a real-life cautionary tale that exemplifies the powerful negative influences that affect today's youth and the consequences that arise from poor choices.

Young Jamila grew up in a loving middle class home, raised by two hardworking parents, the Davises, in the suburbs of Jamaica Queens, New York. Determined to afford their children the luxuries that they themselves never had, the Davises provided their children with a good life, hoping to guarantee their children's success.

At first it seemed as though their formula worked. Young Jamila maintained straight As and became her parents ideal "star child," as she graced the stage of Lincoln Center's Avery Fischer Hall in dance recitals and toured the country in a leading role in an off-Broadway play. All was copacetic in the Davis household until high school years when Jamila met her first love Craig- a 16 year old drug dealer from the Southside housing projects of Jamaica Queens.

As this high school teen rebels, breaking loose from her parents' tight reins, the Davises wage an "all-out" battle to save their only daughter whom they love so desperately. But Jamila is in too deep! Poisoned by the thorn of materialism, she lusts after independence, power and notoriety, and she chooses life in the fast lane to claim them.

When this good girl goes bad, it seems there is no turning back! Follow author, Jamila T. Davis (creator of the Voices of Consequences Enrichment Series) in her trailblazing memoir, *She's All Caught Up!*

ISBN: 978-09855807-3-5
www.voicesbooks.com

NOW AVAILABLE FROM

VOICES

INTERNATIONAL PUBLICATIONS

"Is it fair that corporate giants get to blame 'small fries' like myself, whom they recruited but they walk away scott-free?"
— Jamila T. Davis

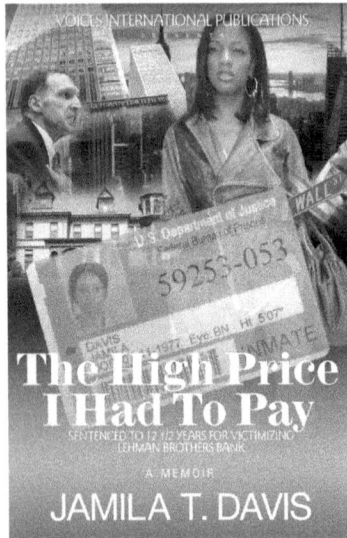

Years before the 2008 Financial Crisis, a major epidemic of mortgage fraud surged throughout the country. The FBI geared up to combat the problem, imprisoning thousands who were alleged to have victimized Wall Street giants, such as Lehman Brothers Bank. Hidden safely behind the auspices of being a "victim," savvy Ivy League bank executives created additional fraudulent schemes to further their profit. Utilizing their "victimizers" as scapegoats, the bankers' clever plan went undetected. Consequently, the real architects of the massive fraudulent lending schemes escaped unpunished. And the "small fries," who the bankers blamed to be the bandits, were left to do big time!

The High Price I Had To Pay is a captivating real-life story that reveals another aspect of the inside fraud perpetrated by Lehman executives that has yet to be told!

This illuminating synopsis by author Jamila T. Davis, who is currently serving a 12 1/2 year sentence in federal prison for bank fraud, is shared from a unique stand point. Davis was labeled by Lehman attorneys as the 25 year old mastermind who devised an elaborate mortgage scheme that defrauded their bank of 22 million dollars. Her shocking story captures the inside tricks of Wall Street elite and takes you up-close and personal into a world driven by greed and power.

Davis' story will leave you amazed and make you think. Have savvy Wall Street executives, such as Richard Fuld, been able to out smart the world? And while these executives escape unpunished, is it fair that "small fries," like Davis, are left to do big time?

ISBN: 978-09855807-9-7
www.voicesbooks.com

"To-date, I have served 16 years of the 30 year sentence that was handed down to me. I feel like I was left here to die, sort of like being buried alive!"
— Jamila T. Davis

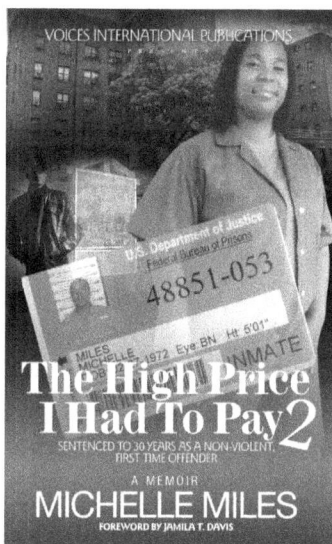

In 1982, during a period when illegal drug use was on the decline, President Ronald Reagan officially announced the War on Drugs. In support of his effort, Congress passed bills to tremendously increase the sentences imposed on drug dealers, including lengthy mandatory minimum sentences. With drug sentences accounting for the majority of the increase, in less than 30 years, the U.S. prison population exploded from 300,000 to more than 2 million! The statistics are well known, but the true faces of those imprisoned and the effects of their incarceration is less publicized.

The High Price I Had To Pay 2, is a captivating real-life story about the life of Michele Miles, a 21 year old, African American woman, who grew up in Marcy Housing Project in Brooklyn, New York. Miles lured in by her boyfriend, Stanley Burrell, tried her hand in the drug game, as a way to escape poverty. Through what she believed to be a promising opportunity, Miles became partners in the notorious "Burrell Organization," which became a thriving enterprise. Overnight, Miles went from "rags-to-riches." In her mind, she was living the life of her dreams.

All was well until the FEDS got wind of the operation. With the help of informants, the Burrell empire swiftly crumbled and the key players were arrested, including Miles. In the end, her role in the drug conspiracy led Miles to receive a thirty year sentence in federal prison.

Miles' story gives readers an inside view of the life of women serving hefty sentences for drug crimes, and the effects of their incarceration. This story will leave you shocked about the rules of prosecution for drug offenders in the U.S. judicial system and make you think. Should a first time, non-violent offender, receive a thirty year sentence?

ISBN: 978-09911041-0-9
www.voicesbooks.com

"I am a 73 Year Old woman currently serving an 11 year sentence in federal prison. One bad decision landed me a decade plus sentence as a first time, non-violent offender."
— Gwendolyn Hemphill

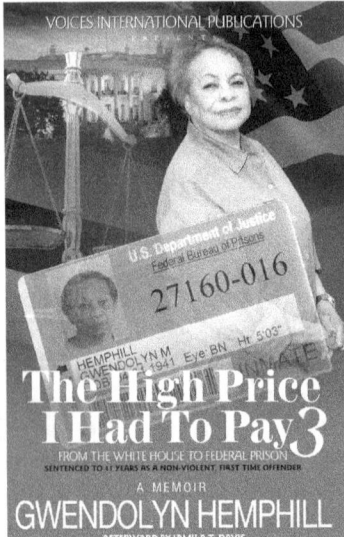

The High Price
I Had To Pay 3
FROM THE WHITE HOUSE TO FEDERAL PRISON
SENTENCED TO 11 YEARS AS A NON-VIOLENT, FIRST TIME OFFENDER
A MEMOIR
GWENDOLYN HEMPHILL

Since 1970, the U.S. prison population has increased seven fold, growing to over 2 million prisoners. Consequently, even though it only consists of 5% of the world's population, America leads the world with the largest prison population. Crime rates are not increasing, yet the U.S. prison population continues to steadily grow. As a result, mass incarceration is a major epidemic that destroys families and costs tax payers billions of dollars each year. The statistics are well known, but the true faces of those imprisoned and the injustices they encounter in the U.S. judicial system is less publicized.

The High Price I Had To Pay, Volume 3, is a captivating true story about the life of Gwendolyn Hemphill, a 73 year old woman currently serving a 11 year sentence for her role in a scheme to defraud the Washington Teachers Union (WTU).

Rising from humble beginnings in the rural town of Johnstown, Pennsylvania, Hemphill worked relentlessly to overcome barriers of poverty and racism. Known for her savvy wit and creative political strategies, she successfully advocated for unions and political groups, including the legendary SNCC, during the era of the civil rights movement. Climbing to the top of the political ladder, as a rising star, Hemphill made her way up to the White House under the Carter Administration. For decades, she vigorously served as a liaison who provided substantial contributions to her community; making waves in the world of Washington D.C. politics. Despite her accomplishments and her stellar career, one bad decision landed Hemphill a decade plus sentence in federal prison, as a first time, non-violent offender.

Hemphill's story gives readers and inside view of the many female, white collar offenders, who are serving lengthy sentences behind bars. This story will leave you questioning is there mercy and equality for all citizens in the U.S. judicial system? And, it will make you think: Should a senior citizen with a stellar past serve a decade plus sentence as a first time, non-violent offender?

ISBN: 978-0-9911041-2-3
www.voicesbooks.com

VOICES
INTERNATIONAL PUBLICATIONS

ORDER FORM

Mail to: 196-03 Linden Blvd.
St. Albans, NY 11412
or visit us on the web @
www.vocseries.com

QTY	Title	Price
	Unlocking the Prison Doors	14.95
	Unlocking the Prison Doors Workbook/Journal	14.95
	Permission to Dream	14.95
	Permission to Dream Workbook/Journal	14.95
	Pursuit to A Greater "Self"	14.95
	Pursuit to A Greater "Self" Workbook/Journal	14.95
	High Price I Had To Pay Volumes 1-3	7.99
	She's All Caught Up	14.95
	Total For Books	
	20% Inmate Discount -	
	Shipping/Handling +	
	Total Cost	

* Shipping/Handling 1-3 books 4.95
    4-9 books 8.95
* Incarcerated individuals receive a 20% discount on each book purchase.
* Forms of Accepted Payments: Certified Checks, Institutional Checks and Money Orders.
* Bulk rates are available upon requests for orders of 10 books or more.
* Curriculum Guides are available for group sessions.
* All mail-in orders take 5-7 business days to be delivered. For prison orders, please
    allow up to (3) three weeks for delivery.

SHIP TO:

Name: _____

Address: _____

_____

City: _____

State: _____ Zip: _____

www.ingramcontent.com/pod-product-compliance
Lightning Source LLC
LaVergne TN
LVHW051520080426
835509LV00017B/2136